Advance Praise for *Culture Connection*

"*The best path to achieving a sustainable competitive advantage in a dynamic marketplace is through the development of an innovative and winning corporate culture. In building and optimising a leading culture, an organization can significantly differentiate their brand in the hearts and minds of their customers, employees and communities whilst delivering meaningful value appreciation for shareholders. Marty Parker has captured a compelling collection of corporate culture insights and learnings in this book, making it a great tool for leaders at all levels in profit-based, charitable and government organizations alike. Marty truly gets it that culture is the ultimate competitive advantage*".

—DARREN ENTWISTLE, President and CEO, TELUS Corporation

"*Marty Parker is the Wayne Gretzky of corporate culture. In his book* Culture Connection, *he builds a clear and credible case for the significance of culture as a primary source of competitive advantage. Marty has studied performance-based cultures and built a very successful business helping organizations identify human capital which contributes to a performance-based culture. This book is a practical and fascinating source for any leader interested in the art and science of building a performance-based culture*".

—PAUL ALOFS, President and CEO,
The Princess Margaret Hospital Foundation

"*Marty Parker has interviewed a virtual who's who of North American industry and applied their collective experience to produce a book brimming with advice and strategies on how to build a winning corporate culture.*"

—DOUGLAS KELLY, Publisher, *National Post*

"*Marty Parker's* Culture Connection *is a must-read for all leaders who shape teams for high performance—be it a small or large corporation,* a department, a soccer team or a non-profit. Having been part of McKinsey, FedEx and, now, Purolator, I know first-hand how excellence starts with people and shaping a corporate culture. I wish I had had Marty Parker's nuggets and insights earlier. They are the perfect thought and action starters on shaping a world-class team".

— TOM SCHMITT, President and CEO, Purolator Inc.

"This is a very readable and illustrative book on what it takes to have a great corporate culture. The companies referenced in this book show how they not only engage people's minds . . . but most importantly their hearts".

— MIKE WILSON, CEO, Agrium

"Marty Parker has been a champion for the importance of corporate culture for many years, and in Culture Connection he brings together his knowledge and passion for the subject with clear evidence that developing and maintaining a high performance culture is, in fact, the only sustainable competitive advantage".

— JIM TRELIVING, Chairman and Owner,
Boston Pizza International Inc.

"Marty Parker's work brings to the forefront the critical role that culture plays in driving business success".

— JOHN CROCKER, President and CEO, HOOPP
(Healthcare of Ontario Pension Plan)

"Marty Parker captures and articulates one of the least talked about but most important aspects of corporate success, and it is about time that someone treated corporate culture as a business metric rather than treating it as some airy-fairy concept. It is the foundation of any business success, and not simply window dressing. Not only does this book identify that fact, Marty's step-by-step approach provides a terrific paint-by-numbers guide as to how to build the strongest possible culture while being able to recognize and ward off the threats to it. When business students are finished reading about present values, statistics and long-run marginal cost curves, they should stop, shut off the computer, breathe, and realize that none of that matters unless they understand the basics of this book".

— LEONARD ASPER, President and CEO, Sygnus Corp.

"Corporate culture, in fact any culture, is always a work in progress. It's a journey; and the trip is happening whether we pay attention to it or not! In Culture Connection, Marty Parker does a great job of reinforcing that, as senior leaders, it pays to give culture as much attention as we give strategy and systems. In fact, aligning all three is essential—as Marty says, 'either you control your culture, or your culture will control you'. By extracting from real-life and current examples from his many years working with some of Canada's best organizations, Marty provides pragmatic advice for leaders on how to grow the culture we want. Culture Connection is a great addition to the literature on corporate culture that I'm sure organizational leaders will find very useful no matter where they are on their corporate cultural journey".

—MAURICE TULLOCH, President and CEO, Aviva Canada Inc.

"Marty Parker has captured key insights into how corporate culture can be an instrument of resilience in chaos, or corporate transformation for improved performance".

—SAM SHAW, Vice President, Natural Gas
Policy Development, Encana

"This is an exceptionally helpful book. Marty Parker has created a wonderful collection of quotes, examples and anecdotes from some of the most successful companies in the world. These stories will help you benchmark your company culture against the very best and help you get started on shifting your culture to make your company even more effective, regardless of your starting point".

—TIM PENNER, Retired President, Procter & Gamble Canada

"'Corporate culture is the single greatest asset driving performance'. I believe. I believe. I believe. Culture Connection convinces us of this truth, while at the same time, gives us, as leaders, practical, hands-on tactics to consider as we define and build our corporate cultures. It is compelling reading—well written, relevant, personal and helpful. Marty writes with such an intimate and personal style. This is a must-read for all leaders of organizations everywhere"!

—KELLY MURUMETS, President and CEO, ParticipACTION

"In business, corporate culture is often not well understood and it's overlooked. Once you understand how the power of great corporate culture can help your business you are well on your way to success. This book not only outlines what great corporate culture looks like, but it also provides insights from some of North America's greatest business leaders on how they have used corporate culture to build their businesses".

— MIKE CORDOBA, CEO, Empresario Capital

"In my experience, which includes the turnaround of three historical department stores, I have learned firsthand, and concur with Marty's findings, that there is a direct relationship between culture and performance that translates to profit".

— BONNIE BROOKS, President and Chief Executive Officer, The Bay

"Understanding how to develop a superior corporate culture is one of the most important activities of organizations these days. Marty shares the insight he has developed through his exposure to organizations with leading corporate cultures. His perspective provides the basic ingredients that will help you begin your journey to a winning corporate culture".

— PIERRE-YVES JULIEN, President and CEO, Medavie Blue Cross

"Organizational culture matters. In fact, a great one may boost your business performance by 600% according to the extensive research in Culture Connection. Today's competitive economic environment will always eat up firms with inadequate leadership, behaviours, intellectual capital and systems. The true inimitable advantage for business is getting that formula bang on. In this book, Marty Parker takes you on an enjoyable journey through the cultural landscape of some of Canada's top performing companies. You will learn unique insights from leading corporate leaders delivered in an eloquent package. You will definitely re-read this book time and time again. So for this reason, be sure to position your copy in a prominent spot on your bookshelf".

— Dr. Nick Bontis, award-winning Professor of Strategic Management at McMaster University and author of *Information Bombardment*

"Marty has worked with leading North American executives, whose strong corporate cultures have outperformed their peers. In Culture

Connection, *Marty presents the essentials of recruiting, development, recognition, leadership, management and corporate responsibility in a manner that develops a winning organizational structure and culture".*

—BILL JONES, President and Owner, Kemrow Company Limited

"I find Marty's philosophy on the value of culture to be both inspirational and instructive. His stories from successful business leaders are not only fascinating but demonstrate that there are many different ways to get it right. Adding to that is his vast interview and placement experience in identifying not only winners, but winners that fit. You cannot build a brand without a clear supportive corporate culture. Brand is not sustainable without culture, and brand can sustain companies through hard times and generations. Emerging leaders such as myself appreciate the insights that Mr. Parker offers in this great book".

—LES MANDELBAUM, Cofounder and President, Umbra

"Finally, a book that demonstrates the path to becoming a high-performing company. Leaders always suspected the answer and this provides the methods along with the proven data. Parker has captured this in an interesting and insightful manner".

—STUART SULS, President and Chief Operating Officer, Mr. Lube Canada

"Marty Parker writes with great clarity and offers compelling insights on creating a winning corporate culture. His book is a mandatory read for those business leaders whose objective is to achieve organizational excellence".

—DR. GERARD SEIJTS, Associate Professor of Organizational Behaviour, Executive Director Ian O. Ihnatowycz Institute for Leadership, The Richard Ivey School of Business

" I applaud Marty for his compelling combination of empirical evidence, expert interviews and thorough analysis. His book is a valuable resource for any organization looking to drive performance and provide their organization with a competitive advantage".

—JOSEPH MAPA, President and CEO, Mount Sinai Hospital, Joseph and Wolf Lebovic Health Complex

"Marty Parker has become a subject matter expert in culture through his excellent work in executive search. All of the great content Marty provides

reinforces Peter Drucker's classic statement 'Company cultures are like country cultures. Never try to change one. Try, instead, to work with what you've got'".

— GARY BURKETT, Managing Director,
Human Resources, FedEx Express Canada

"Marty Parker clearly and passionately articulates why Corporate Culture is a not only a legitimate business discipline for CEOs and human resource departments, but a critical subject matter for all those concerned with the performance of their enterprise, no matter the size. This is a "must read" for executives and managers at all levels. Too often Corporate Culture has been seen as a "soft" requirement or as a nice-to-have. Now the case is clear and supported not only by captivating true stories, but also by well-organized empirical data. Thank you, Marty, for connecting the dots".

— AARON MOSCOE, LL.B, CEO of The Promotional Specialists

"Culture is a tangible and actionable asset in any organization—it doesn't happen on its own. For example, if you incorporate your organization's values into performance appraisals you can assess the 'what' and the 'how' with equal importance in order to create a winning culture".

— MARC TELLIER, President and Chief Executive Officer,
Yellow Media, Inc.

"Marty Parker has done what so many of the high-performing CEOs he writes about did: he identified a need in the marketplace, strategized how to attack it, and then executed with skill and determination. Marty's empirical work on corporate culture is nothing short of groundbreaking, and deserves to be on the reading list of anyone who aspires to be a true leader".

–JOE CHIDLEY, Senior Vice President of Corporate and
Public Affairs at Veritas; former Editor, Canadian Business

"Marty Parker's book on a winning organizational culture is excellent. He was able to lay out a process that explains how to establish a winning culture and how to inspire an entire organization to succeed. He uses examples from across a broad range of sectors so we are all able to recognize aspects of ourselves and what our organizations could desire to be".

— JOHANN OLAV KOSS, President and CEO, Right To Play

CULTURE
CONNECTION

CULTURE CONNECTION

HOW DEVELOPING A *WINNING CULTURE*
WILL GIVE YOUR ORGANIZATION
A COMPETITIVE ADVANTAGE

MARTY PARKER

New York   Chicago   San Francisco   Lisbon   London
Madrid   Mexico City   Milan   New Delhi   San Juan
Seoul   Singapore   Sydney   Toronto

1 2 3 4 5 6 7 8 9 10   DOC/DOC   1 9 6 5 4 3 2 1

ISBN 978-0-07-178876-2
MHID 0-07-178876-X

e-ISBN 978-0-07-178877-9
e-MHID 0-07-178877-8

McGraw-Hill products are available at special quantity discounts to use as premiums and sales promotions or for use in corporate training programs. To contact a representative, please e-mail us at bulksales@mcgraw-hill.com.

This book is printed on acid-free paper.

"A daughter may outgrow your lap,
but she will never outgrow your heart."
—Anonymous

To my three beautiful daughters: Jaiden, Corsen,
and Kaelen. You are the inspiration for everything I do,
and I will love you always.

Contents

Acknowledgments

I NEVER BELIEVED THAT I would ever write a book. And now that this one is published, I know that that remains true: this book became a reality because of the work of many, not one.

Writing a book takes a great deal of support and teamwork, and this one was no exception. I have been blessed to have been a member of a lot of great teams, but the team behind this effort is by far the best. While I have dedicated my life's work to building great companies through executive search and cultural assessment, this work will, I hope, allow me to share what I have learned about the greatest organizational asset in existence: culture. But there are many to whom I owe enormous gratitude for making this happen.

I would like to start by thanking the great people of Waterstone Human Capital. Our firm has prospered because of their dedication, commitment, and passion for excellence. Through our work, we have been quietly building great companies and literally changing the lives of the people in these organizations.

The Waterstone board of directors includes Steve Parker, Mike Cordoba, and Don Babick. These exceptional leaders have lent their support to our firm for many years, and their vision and wisdom have been the guiding forces behind Waterstone. This book was as much their brainchild as anyone else's; they believed that it could be done and that it would make a difference. They are three of the smartest people I know, and I am forever grateful to each of them.

The clients of Waterstone are the lifeblood of our firm, and I must thank them all for their loyalty and support, and, most important, for trusting us to help them recruit for fit and build great organizations.

Many thanks to the winners, nominees, partners, and sponsors of our Canada's 10 Most Admired Corporate Cultures program, as well as to all of those who participate in our annual Canadian Corporate Culture Study and Corporate Culture Summit. Canada's 10 and these initiatives have provided us with a living R&D lab that has allowed Waterstone to be at the forefront of best practices in cultural assessment and recruitment for fit.

A great many thanks to all of those who agreed to be interviewed for this book. There are too many of you to mention, but your contribution has been substantial and is greatly appreciated.

If you do break the spine of this book, you will see that I refer to my siblings and my parents frequently. There is a reason for that, as they have given me love, knowledge, wisdom, and unwavering support. To my siblings, Steve, Karl, Calvin, Neil, and Norma, and to my parents, Mary and Norman: I have no words to express my thanks and my love for each and all of you, and I thank you for your support. To Shirley, Allison, and Wayne: thanks for enriching my life with your love and guidance.

I dedicate this book to my three daughters, Jaiden, Corsen, and Kaelen. They are the greatest gifts I have ever received. Thank you for believing in me always. Thank you for making me want to make you proud, and for bringing me joy each and every day. I hope the culture that we have created together for our family brings you great strength, great independence, and, most of all, love and acceptance.

Almost three years ago, I met the most wonderful partner, Tanya, and along with her came two of the most wonderful boys, my stepsons Blair and Braeden. Tanya, thank you for allowing me to try to "do it all" and for convincing me that I can. I hope I am as loving and supportive to you as you are to me.

The greatest thanks I owe is to Jennifer Mondoux. Jennifer is Waterstone's director of marketing and communications, and she is a pillar of wisdom, support, and excellence. She embodies everything we are as a firm: she is humble, professional, driven, and wise. More than anyone, Jennifer made this book happen. She crafted the voice from my words and made sense of all of my interviews with CEOs and leaders across North America. She worked tirelessly, under many deadlines, to make this book a reality. Not only is Jennifer a great writer, but she is also a great person. She is a beacon of good judgment, and she has a wonderful sense of humour. She also cares deeply about doing great work. Jennifer is what great culture is all about—great people. Many thanks to her husband, Kevin, and to her son, Jack, for allowing Jennifer the time and space to help drive this work. And what's more, she has done all this while pregnant with her second child. Jennifer, thank you for helping make this process go seamlessly and for making everything you touch great.

Introduction

I AM THE YOUNGEST OF SIX KIDS. My five siblings were born within a short nine years, and then I came along—nine years later. So there was quite a divide. In fact, my eldest sibling, my brother Steve, is 18 years older than I; he was an adult by the time I was born.

Growing up in Barrie, north of Toronto, I often felt that my natural role in the family was that of observer; I observed the behaviour of my brothers and my sister as they went from being teenagers to being young adults, as well as the behaviour of my parents. I was constantly surrounded by people—typically older people, whether it was my siblings and their friends or my parents (who were well into their forties by the time I was a toddler) and their own, older, siblings.

In the Parker household, our lives centered around five things: music, sports, family, school, and church. We were also a family that was heavily involved in our community. For my mother, and for all of us, that meant the Roman Catholic Church. For me, it also meant school musical productions, the choir, and, of course, team sports—from high school through university, I was coaching and playing in competitive-level baseball, fastball, hockey, track and field, rugby, basketball, and football (and higher levels of football and of track and field after that). I was constantly being coached, constantly being mentored and being exposed to different styles of leadership, and constantly observing the behaviour of others—

whether it was at home, at school, in church, on the stage, on the ice, or on the field.

When you're in the position I was in, as the youngest by far in a much older family, emulating, mimicking, and following the behaviour that you're observing becomes second nature—especially if it's the kind of behaviour that's being recognized and rewarded by parents and other loved ones. It's a great place to be: to have those kinds of guideposts and, in some cases, to be able to define your own behaviour by observing that of other key individuals and loved ones in your life. Over time, you start to develop a really good sense of what makes people successful and what doesn't—at least in terms of your own family's behaviour and values.

So when I first started contemplating the idea of becoming an executive search professional in the latter part of the 1990s, the idea of both observing and making judgment calls on the behaviour of others—which is really, in my view, what a search professional does when assessing a potential candidate on behalf of a client—felt like a natural, and logical, place for me to be.

In many ways, it felt like coming home.

When I founded Waterstone Human Capital almost 10 years ago, I positioned the firm as one that would excel at uncovering our clients' corporate cultures, so that we, as executive search professionals, could recruit the best people to fit those cultures. Throughout my life, I'd found a way to fit into my peer groups by studying what made the highest achievers in those groups successful. When I started in the executive search business, this continued to be my approach. So why not build a company and a practice on the idea of recruiting for fit? We had no idea at the time how significant the demand would be. We also were surprised at the need for cultural assessments for leadership teams, either for companies that were assessing acquisition targets or for those organizations that were simply trying to gain a better understanding of their own culture.

Overview

We've called this book *Culture Connection* because in it, we will show you how culture is a strategic competitive advantage that can set your organization apart from its peers. It will show you how culture directly connects with and drives performance. Case studies and interviews with leading executives, along with a step-by-step guide for hiring for fit and other best practices and leading trends, will demonstrate how culture has been used as a tool to drive performance, at home and abroad, in emerging and established organizations alike.

Here's how the book breaks down:

In Chapters 1–5, we examine how culture, in truly high-performing organizations, starts with a defined set of behaviours or the values that govern them—behaviours that are then reinforced, communicated and aligned throughout the organization. And what drives those behaviours is leadership. In this first part of the book, we also make the case that the successful people who are currently in your organization are the key to finding the right kind of new talent—talent that will drive performance. Critically, we also examine the key role of cultural alignment. In fact, if an organization aligns its systems—through performance management, leadership, compensation, recognition, celebration, training and development, organizational history, company structure, and corporate social responsibility—the systems will align to the culture. Why? Because everything you're then doing as an organization, whether it is conscious or unconscious, will fit in with who you are.

In Chapters 6–14, we look at other specific tactics for aligning culture, including the critical role of training. Here, we make the argument that organizations can train certain behaviours, and not just train for skill. We examine how organizations can use culture to change systems, habits and people; how to recognize culture killers and save your organization from lackluster performance; the importance of culture champions within your organization; and, how credos and belief statements can reinforce culture. We also look at how cultural assessments are the most effective way to identify the critical behaviours shared in a company and how the results gleaned can better arm organizations with information when considering expansion or M&As. Finally, we examine the critical role of the board in both supporting and reinforcing culture within organizations.

In Chapters 15–18, we take an in-depth look at the symbiotic relationship between culture and brand—in that, to build a winning organization, your brand and culture should be one and the same. We will also examine two other key human elements of a successful culture in this final section of the book: first, we'll look at how your organization can recruit for fit and build a high-performance culture by focusing on seven key practices for successful candidate placements. Second, we'll cover how to incorporate best practices in performance management for fit, so that employees, managers and leaders in your organization understand that their success in the company is dependent on *how* they do things, not just *what* they do. Finally, in our last chapter, we'll take a look at the years of research findings from our firm's Canada's 10 Most Admired Corporate Cultures program, as well as from our annual Canadian Corporate Culture Study, to show how culture truly impacts organizational performance.

Successful Leadership

Corporate culture is defined by behaviour. It's how people—meaning the collective of people—in an organization do things. Ideology, vision, mission, and values—these things set the tone. But culture is really about how people behave day-in and day-out. And leadership drives that behaviour. Consider this: from the time our firm started its annual Canadian Corporate Culture Study almost eight years ago, the percentage of respondents who believe that leadership has led to the evolution of their organization's corporate culture has increased from 35 percent in 2006 to 92 percent in 2011.

So what makes some leaders good at what they do and others not? Why do some high performers excel in certain circumstances and others fail, even when they clearly have the right skill set?

It really comes down to fit. Or, to put it another way, if a leader is to be successful, her behaviours need to match the behaviours of the other successful leaders in that group. If those behaviours don't match, a disconnect occurs.

Our work at Waterstone has been about the applied practice of this. We have seen that there are certain high performers who have found a way to be successful in a group dynamic and that there are clear behavioural themes that link those performers to that success. Furthermore, those themes are typically set and accepted by the organization's leadership (and, more important, *represented* by that leadership).

A winning corporate culture doesn't develop in a vacuum. The really great, high-performing organizations and their leaders purposely define behaviours and align the interests of their people with the interests of the company, much the way families do. This certainly was the case in my household when I was growing up: the leadership of an extraverted mother who possessed strong Christian values and was involved in the Roman Catholic community; an extremely hard-working, doting, introverted, but supportive father whose values aligned with those of our mother; and all of my older siblings, who represented those same behaviours in their own unique way. It was an environment in which achievements, collaboration, respect for authority, and hard work were recognized. The defined behaviours in our family defined our success.

I remember a high school girlfriend once saying to me, "I don't understand how you can fit in with the artsy kids and the jocks." The thing is, I never really thought about trying to. I never talked to the artsy kids about sports; I just liked art—I liked painting; I liked music; I liked dance. I wanted to know what made them great at what they did. It became a fascination with me, even at that stage of my life. Instead of just accepting that some people are good at certain things and some aren't, I wanted to know why. What makes some good and others great? What do they have? What makes them fit in? Why can they be successful in one environment and not the other?

I now know that the answers to these questions lie in organizational culture and what is expected and accepted as the norms of behaviour.

It only took me about 30 years to figure it out.

Chapter 1

Know Thyself

Know thyself.

—SOCRATES

THE LEADERS OF CORPORATE Canada don't usually stand on their chairs and cheer—and certainly not at stuffy awards dinners.

But this was no stuffy awards dinner. From the get-go, we had deliberately gone in the opposite direction for our Canada's 10 Most Admired Corporate Cultures awards gala: we wanted the night to be fun. More important, our objective was for the program's annual winners to "show off their culture" at the event—to bring out their teams and celebrate. And boy, did they ever . . .

So there I was, in February of 2010, in the sold-out ballroom of the Four Seasons Hotel Toronto, standing on my chair like the rest of the 500 willing participants. From the stage, Patch Evans, CEO of Goodlife Fitness (one of Canada's 10 winners in 2009), led our audience through a signature element of Goodlife's corporate culture: a ritual at all employee gatherings called the Margarita. Part motivational cheer and part physical stretch, the end result of the Margarita is the reinforcement of the company's brand, "I'm Sexy, Smart and Strong".

1

Who'd have thought that Canada's leading CEOs and senior HR leaders would be standing on chairs with their hands waving in the air, shouting that phrase at the top of their lungs, at an awards dinner on a Monday night in Toronto in February?

To me, it was yet another reinforcement of a belief that we've had for quite a while in our executive search practice: culture matters to successful organizations. But culture is more than company foosball tables, in-house gyms, and nifty lunchrooms. Culture matters precisely because (and we have proven this) it leads to great performance. In fact, organizations with clearly defined, easily communicated, and well-aligned cultures win in the marketplace and outperform their peers.

Ten years ago, no one thought much about corporate culture. The term was barely used. In fact, as a new search firm back in the early 2000s, the marketing research consultants that we hired advised us to "not go down the culture road". Even our own board of directors warned that we might be going at this alone and that this type of positioning, although noble, might not be the ideal place to stake our claim. Thankfully, our search experience at the time was providing us with enough anecdotal evidence to ignore all of that advice.

What were we seeing? Clients were putting a higher weighting on "fit" in the hiring process. And the candidates we placed, those who were hired for having the right kinds of behaviours—the same behaviours that defined success at the client's organization—were more successful and had longer tenures than the ones who were hired strictly for their skill set. The dynamics became clear to us: we realized that in order to do great work in executive search, we needed to understand the culture of an organization and what makes its high performers, high performers.

Clearly, culture is more than an employee group cheer. It's about how people behave, day in and day out. In fact, in truly high-performing organizations, culture starts with a defined set of behaviours or the values that govern them—behaviours that are then reinforced, communicated, and aligned throughout the organization. And driving those behaviours is leadership.

Great organizations, like our annual group of Canada's 10 Most Admired Corporate Cultures, exercise the principle that I'll call "Know Thyself". This knowledge often begins with a frank assessment of the organization's existing culture—which may not have always been a great one.

In fact, cultural assessments (the fastest area of growth in our business) often happen because an existing culture is not well defined, is misunderstood, or is verging on dysfunctionality. But sometimes the situation is not nearly as dire as this. Often, an organization's culture may simply be in need of definition rather than improvement. In any event, knowing thyself begins with assessing your culture. The objectives are to clearly define that culture—and, most important, to articulate it—and to find new and systematic ways to use your culture to unleash the power of your people to perform. With knowledge and understanding come great power.

Knowing thyself also means taking that assessment and driving its outcomes throughout the organization. It means defining the behaviours that should be rewarded and recognized, and aligning those behaviours throughout your organization's HR systems. It also means understanding how your high performers perform and recruiting new leaders based on that knowledge. As we'll learn in Chapter 16, "Recruiting for Fit", finding successful people isn't enough anymore—it's finding out how they're successful that's really important. In fact, the successful people who are currently in your organization are the key to finding the right kind of new talent. In our practice, this is exactly how we approach executive search. Why? Because it consistently leads to the right hire.

The ultimate outcome of the Know Thyself principle is great performance; it's the first step towards that goal. I'll come right out and say it: culture is the single greatest asset that an organization can have. If you don't believe me, take a look at the numbers. We've proven the impact of culture on performance each year through our Canada's 10 Most Admired Corporate Cultures program. For instance, in terms of a three-year compound annual growth rate, our 2010 winners outpaced the S&P/TSX 60 by an average of nearly 600 percent—or six times.[1] And no matter what year we measure this, our Canada's 10 consistently outpace Canada's biggest and best.

Isn't that something to cheer about?

Culture and Values at Maple Leaf Foods

Let's talk about the recent history of Maple Leaf Foods, a leading food processing company headquartered in Toronto that employs 21,000 people in its operations across Canada and in the United States, the United Kingdom, and Asia, and that had sales of $5.0 billion in 2010.[2]

In October of 1998, Michael McCain, then president and COO of Maple Leaf Foods, slid a piece of paper across the table to Wayne Johnson, his (now retired) senior vice president and chief human resources officer. On it, he said, were a list of 21 values that McCain had drafted himself. As he was about to become CEO in January of the following year, McCain told Johnson that cultural change was coming to Maple Leaf Foods, and to make that happen, these were the values he wanted implemented.

As the list came across the table, Johnson rolled his eyes.

"Michael challenged me, and he said, 'What are you rolling your eyes for?'" Johnson told me when we sat down for an interview together. "I said that I'd had some experience where CEOs had tried to do this, and it had failed because it wasn't a good representation of what the CEO stood for, and when you boiled it all down, culture is really driven by the way your boss acts."

After quickly scanning the list, however, Johnson nodded and said that the values would be easy to implement.

"I think that infuriated him even more, and so he said, 'Why the change of mind?' And I said, 'Because this is the way you behave, and so it's believable and we can sell it'", said Johnson.

"He strongly believes, and he is absolutely right, that culture starts at the top and that the CEO has to own the culture".

What emerged from that discussion is what Maple Leaf Foods refers to as the two key components of its cultural DNA. The first is the Leadership Edge, a program based on the idea that leadership drives a company's success, as demonstrated through its 21 stated values (and the behaviours that support them), which include "Do What's Right" and "Be Performance Driven". Second, Six Sigma, a management operating system guided by the organization's values, which assigns "black belts", or project leaders, to initiatives that are the business's top priority and are actively championed by senior leaders in the organization.[3]

If you follow Maple Leaf Foods, you'll know that the organization faced a serious and devastating crisis in August of 2008 when a number of Maple Leaf deli meats were found to be contaminated with listeria, a type of bacterium that infects humans. The contamination led to the deaths of 22 people and made many others ill.[4]

In fact, the organization was hammered with the perfect storm in that year and the following, being faced not only with the fallout from the crisis but also with rising commodity prices and an economic downturn. Despite all this, at the end of October 2009, Maple Leaf Foods reported a net income of $22.5 million compared to a net loss of $12.9 million in the previous year.[5]

What saved it?

Maple Leaf Foods' well-defined, proactively communicated, and strongly aligned culture, combined with an outstanding CEO at the helm who lives the culture and walks the talk, is the reason why the organization survived and thrived through what was arguably the toughest time in its history. To put it in a simpler way, I think Maple Leaf Foods survived the perfect storm because its leadership has mastered the principle of Know Thyself and driven it—aligned it—throughout the organization in various concrete ways. A year after the crisis, on the one-year anniversary of the tragedy, Maple Leaf Foods took out full-page ads in major Canadian dailies. Framed as a letter to consumers from McCain himself, the message reinforced that Maple Leaf Foods would never forget what had happened and was committed to ensuring that this tragedy would never happen again.

If this doesn't exemplify how great leaders "walk the talk", I don't know what does. Here was McCain, a year after the listeria crisis, still dealing with the professional fallout and the associated personal stress. But he continued to behave as the perfect embodiment of the Maple Leaf Leadership Values. Is it any wonder that "Do What's Right", "Dare to Be Transparent", and "Communicating Candidly, and in a Direct Manner" are on that list?

No kidding. McCain wrote those values himself.

Great leaders, like McCain, openly and publicly embody the ideals and values of the company; they have enormous influence in setting the tone for an organization. In many ways they are the guardians of culture.

As a whole new set of challenges faces Maple Leaf Foods in 2011, including the ongoing fallout from the Ontario Teachers' Pension Plan Board selling its remaining stake in Maple Leaf at a discount in November

2010, weaker sales, higher ingredient prices, and a higher Canadian dollar,[6] it remains to be seen how the organization will continue to perform. Will its culture continue to be what saves it in tough times? With its plans to focus on real and lasting changes in the profitability of the business, including restructuring to cut costs, the introduction of new products, and targeting health-conscious consumers—and, most important, the constant communication of these new tactics by McCain himself—my hunch is yes. Why? Because McCain will employ the same behavioural characteristics and leadership style in dealing with future challenges as he has in dealing with everything else.

Corporate Culture as a Foundation

I once sat across from a very intelligent CEO who said to me, "I'm not sure we really have a culture that can be defined", and I remember thinking, "How do I share with him that every organization has a culture? You just have to know what it is". Corporate culture is a critical foundation of any organization. A strong, healthy culture drives performance and helps organizations withstand anything that's thrown at them. A weak and dysfunctional culture is a liability that exposes organizations and makes them vulnerable when times are tough.

With respect to your own organization, ask yourself these questions: Do you know your own culture? Can you articulate it? Is your culture "okay", but not great? Is cultural change needed? If you know that your culture is weak, but the organization is still performing, is the performance sustainable under those circumstances? Is the impetus for change there?

Most business leaders can appreciate that culture affects the functioning of the organization. However, there's a slightly condescending view—surprisingly, still predominantly held in the media as well—that culture is a nice-to-have, and that it revolves mostly around things like posted company values, flextime work arrangements, and the aforementioned foosball tables. But if you take that view, you're missing the mark—completely.

Culture is a competitive advantage. It should be viewed as a weapon in your company's arsenal, because when it is properly defined and aligned throughout an organization, it will become a performance driver. Strategy, products, and tactics—all of these things can be copied, to a certain extent. But culture can't be copied. Like DNA, it's a nonrepeatable marker setting your organization apart from everyone else.

That's what this conversation is about.

Figuring out how to uncover, evaluate, and improve your culture, in order to align it with your business goals, can be a bit baffling—in fact, it stumps many. That's why the cultural assessment is so important, and why it's such a great starting point.

It comes back to the Know Thyself principle: until you examine your organization's culture in detail, you're operating in a vacuum.

Here's how you start.

Carry Out a Cultural Assessment

Every organization's corporate culture can be assessed, and the insights gleaned from that assessment can be used to improve organizational performance.

Think of a cultural assessment as a self-reflection, allowing you to take a deep dive in—to examine the existing values and behaviours of your organization, and also how those values and behaviours align with where you are trying to go as a company. From there, the objective is to determine if—and where—there are gaps.

Regardless of what you do with it, a cultural assessment can provide insights into how your company works, both as a whole and by functional area. Whether you do the assessment yourself or have someone else do it for you, the findings of your assessment—the outcomes—need to be supported by either a set of recommendations or a course of action.

Sometimes the outcome can be quite specific.

When a client of ours in the financial services sector decided to undergo a cultural assessment with us, it did so because it wanted to understand how its people defined their culture. The client also wanted to get a better understanding of the issues it was experiencing with respect to cultural alignment. In fact, through the assessment process, the company discovered that recruitment—specifically, hiring for fit rather than hiring primarily based on skill, which was what it had been and which was leading to bad hires—should be the key platform for strengthening its culture.

This is a great example of how an assessment can reveal an untapped aspect of your organization's culture.

To use an analogy, cultural assessments are like physicals. If you're a pretty healthy person and you have no interest in living beyond your normal life expectancy, you'll stay the course: you'll keep your diet the same, you'll keep your exercise levels the same, and you won't do anything above and beyond what's required to extend your shelf life or improve the quality of it, so to speak. But if you want to live longer and better, and you want more out of that longer life, you're going to do more than what's required. You may exercise more, eat better, and improve your emotional, physical, and mental health in other ways—and it's how you do these things that matters.

Similarly, it's what you do with your cultural assessment that matters.

In any event, for any cultural assessment to truly have an impact, it must be driven from the top—if not by the leader, then by the organization's senior leadership team.

A great example of this is the remarkable story of Four Seasons Hotels and Resorts and its founder and chairman, Isadore Sharp.

The Service Culture at Four Seasons

If you've stayed at a Four Seasons, you'll know that it's an incredible experience. From the moment you walk onto a property, you can't help but notice that every single person working there—the front desk staff, the concierge, the chambermaids, the restaurant staff, everybody—seems to excel at service. It's a remarkable experience for a guest, and it's even more remarkable because this guest experience has stayed the same for 50 years, even as Four Seasons has grown from one hotel to 85 hotels in more than 35 countries.[7]

The idea of building that kind of service culture came on the heels of a tough assessment by Sharp of the company's culture and of its future. In the late 1970s, Sharp made the decision to move the business from what was largely a construction operation engaged in real estate development to a management company focused on creating a group of the world's finest hotels. He then introduced several new concepts to his management team. For instance, the Golden Rule (treat others as you would wish to be treated) became the guiding principle for anyone who worked at the hotel, from how management interacted with employees to how guests were treated. Sharp wanted to empower the frontline staff, enabling them to make decisions on the spot, thus kick-starting the service experience from the moment guests walked in the door. This required a change in management thinking—from seeing employees as a group to be managed and controlled, to a focus on mutual values like respect, fairness, honesty, and trust. In a nutshell, Sharp told his management team to treat employees with the same understanding that they gave the hotel's guests.[8] From this, great service—along with satisfied clients and their repeat business—will ensue. A number of innovations in the hotel business followed. For instance, Four Seasons was the first company to put shampoo in bathrooms, to offer 24-hour room service, and to create floors where smoking was not permitted.[9]

As hard as Sharp sold the Golden Rule, it wasn't always met with enthusiasm by his leadership bench. In fact, there's a great quote in Sharp's 2009 work, *Four Seasons: The Story of a Business Philosophy*, that illustrates both what he was up against and his resolve to fix it:

> *It took most of the first half of the 1980s to clear out all the obstacles that stood in the way of improving service: to part ways with every executive who believed my "kooky" credo should be confined to the PR department, to part ways with every executive whose actions contradicted policy and sabotaged our credibility.*[10]

Talk about intestinal fortitude. In some cases, the decisions were very personal. But the simple fact was that many of these individuals weren't going to be the people who would help teach and sell the hoteliers in the Four Seasons family on Sharp's vision. It paid off, however, and many of the new additions to the management team at that time are running the company today. In fact, if you look at the Four Seasons senior staff tenure list, you'll see that the average number of years of service of management committee members is 22, and seeing 30 or 35 years of service is not uncommon.[11] That kind of loyalty and commitment to the Four Seasons brand, and to its world-renowned service culture, is something that started only because of a deep assessment of what the Four Seasons was and what it wanted to be. For Sharp, that assessment said: the Golden Rule was the basis for moving forward; it was the organization's future.

Conclusion

It's remarkable how the best-in-class organizations that we talk about in this book, like Four Seasons Hotels and Resorts, truly do exemplify the principle of Know Thyself. They've dedicated time and effort to defining who they are, and, as we'll see, they have systematically aligned those defined values and behaviours throughout their organizations. As we'll also see, these same organizations have been able to figure out when and how to evolve their cultures based on a set of ever-changing circumstances.

The most successful corporate cultures are shaped by the leader's own vision of how things should be done and influenced by her actions and behaviours; it's the "tone from the top". Those same leaders will establish behavioural themes — not just for themselves, but for their executive teams. The key is for the leaders to "walk the talk" and to be living, breathing representations of those behavioural themes. Great organizations with strong cultures do this very well.

To truly — and quickly — understand the culture of your organization, and to start establishing those behavioural themes, take a long, hard look at your own high performers. These "stars" exhibit everything you need to know about creating a high-performance culture. By examining their behaviours closely, you'll begin to understand what makes you successful.

Chapter 2

The Answers Are
in the Stars

It isn't what you do,
but how you do it.

—John Wooden

Ferio Pugliese shared this thought with me recently:

Although skills, knowledge, and abilities are very important to
do the job, they're not the success factors that are going to drive
your value proposition and your culture. It's the value fit. I can
have the smartest guy in the world, he can be the best pilot, the
best flight attendant, but if he doesn't fit the value proposition
of wanting to help, wanting to smile, wanting to be friendly,
wanting to be honest, then that doesn't match our brand.

Ferio had invited me to attend one of WestJet's Culture Connection sessions out near Pearson Airport in Toronto, and we were sitting and having coffee before the session started. Pugliese is the senior vice president of people for WestJet, an airline founded in 1996 in Calgary, Alberta, with 200 employees and three aircraft. WestJet now has 7,800 employees; flies its 88 Boeing Next Generation aircraft to 71 destinations in Canada, the United States, the Caribbean, and Mexico; and is aiming to be one of the five most successful international airlines in the world by 2016.[1] Like most "WestJetters", Pugliese is a terrific communicator, and he truly represents the WestJet culture.

If you know anything about WestJet, you'll know how much weight the airline puts on its culture—a culture that we'll learn more about later in the book. The point I'll briefly make here is that from the get-go, WestJet's founders put in place systems—including profit-sharing and share-purchasing plans—that aligned the interests of its people with those of the airline. I've often heard Pugliese proudly say that WestJetters "walk around like they own the place". That's because they do. The culture is based on the principle of caring and providing a great guest experience. And it works because WestJetters are, in fact, owners.

I've shared Pugliese's quote with you because it's a great example of an organization that understands its culture, precisely because it has a crystal-clear understanding of the behaviours that it wants and expects from its people.

As a leader in your organization, do you have that same kind of understanding of the kinds of behaviours you both want and expect to see?

Even more important, do you understand how your top performers behave?

These are critical questions. And if your answer is no, particularly to the second question, you may have a tough time understanding your own culture.

Look at Your Top Performers

We often tell our clients that the best way to get fast information on their culture is to understand the behaviour of their top performers; to interview these individuals and to "map" their behaviours. Admittedly, the first response to that suggested tactic is sometimes a confused one. Clients want to know: How do I this? What are the costs? It must be impossible!

Our response is, "Look up". The answers are in the stars—specifically, the stars within your own organization. Spend time with these high performers, and you'll start to see behavioural patterns. In other words, you'll start to identify the kinds of behaviours that drive success—and that drive performance—in your organization. Alternatively, you may also discover what kind of behaviours are holding your culture back from truly performing.

As recruiters, and as professionals in cultural assessment, behavioural mapping is also where we start. Why? Because it's critical information. We could waste a lot of time in a recruitment effort looking at everyone in the organization, trying to find successful people and determine what the success culture is—but if we focus on the high performers and spend time with them, we'll start to get some answers. If we have an understanding of the kinds of behaviour that drive the success of those specific individuals, we can then begin to understand your culture. Simply put, that information allows us to find the best candidate for the role—to hire for fit. With or without a recruiter on its side, every organization should take this approach. To truly know your culture, look up— look at the stars in your organization. Map and model their behaviour, and you'll have a true understanding of your culture.

We're not alone in thinking this way. In fact, top organizations— like WestJet—also see the advantages of behavioural mapping.

Behavioural Mapping

Behavioural mapping is essentially a type of systematic observational research that tracks behaviour over space and time. It involves spending time with people and looking at their behaviour, ideally over a few meetings and in a variety of different locations. Whereas a cultural assessment is a high-level in-depth look across the entire organization, behavioural mapping is specifically focused on high performers. Most of us can get a pretty good sense of someone after spending an hour or two with him. The point of the mapping exercise, however, is to look for individual, systematic, and repeated behaviours.

Here are some other guidelines:

- Spend time with high performers across the organization's functions, departments, regional offices, and business units. The point here is to gain an understanding of the behaviour of these individuals across the scope of the business.

- Determine how many top performers you should map. We've completed behavioural mapping with only 6 to 8 individuals. Sometimes it takes as many as 25. We've also done it with up to 50 top performers. It all depends on the size of the organization and how detailed you want your mapping to be.
- Detailed assessments would include a broader cross section of individuals, but in the case of high performers, your behavioural mapping exercise should involve middle to senior management as well as all of the key players.
- Look for anywhere from 8 to 10 core behaviours, but don't be married to these numbers. Sometimes 6 behavioural themes will emerge; sometimes there will be as many as 12. Find commonalities involving the high performers of your particular organization — there may be more, or less, than you expect. The key here is to ask these individuals what makes them successful and to observe how they act in different scenarios. As we'll see in Chapter 16, this is also a key tactic when recruiting for fit.

It's one thing to look for commonalities in the behaviour of your top performers. What can be even more insightful, in terms of really knowing your culture, are the clashes. This means, are there competing behaviours on the part of your top performers that can cause tension or problems? Figuring out these behavioural clashes can provide you with key information.

Here are a few examples of behaviours that clash.

1. Social Focus versus Task Focus

Do your top performers excel at pushing decisions through because they are focused on developing and improving relationships, or are they more concerned with simply completing their assigned tasks? In larger organizations, being collaborative and working across departments in order to get things done is critical. Using moral suasion, being influential, getting to know how other roles affect decision making, understanding how busy people are and how they get things done, and other such behaviours are all key traits. Within your leadership team, is the ability to get things done through relationship building more important than merely being task focused? Are these behaviours competing among your top performers? If so, what does it mean for your organization's culture?

2. Individual Focus versus Team Focus

Does your organization want its top performers thinking like team players, or do you want individual stars to emerge? Some organizations are very team-focused, by the nature of what they do. Take Boston Pizza, for example. Incorporated in 1983, Boston Pizza is Canada's number one casual dining brand, with 340 restaurants (and another 60 in the United States) and more than 16,000 employees. The organization lives and breathes by its "Three Pillars of Success": a commitment to franchisee profitability, a commitment to building the Boston Pizza brand, and a commitment to continuously improving the guest experience.[2]

But it's the attention to the franchisees that is incredibly team-focused at Boston Pizza. Area managers, operations staff, and national and regional marketing groups work as a team to support the franchisees.

Why?

When George Melville and Jim Treliving, the chairmen and owners of Boston Pizza, were building their franchisee community, they sold the concept without head leases and without guaranteed bank loans. The result? Out of necessity and based on their own values of respect and trust, Treliving and Melville knew that making franchisees feel important was a key element in their success.

"We knew we had to create a franchisee community that wanted to be a part of us because if they didn't want to stay with us, they could leave", Melville explained to me recently. "Franchisees are our partners; they're our customers. We wanted to create an environment where they wanted to stay. We wanted to have a group that wanted to be together — not a group that was trying to figure out how to get out".

For Treliving, making sure that the Boston Pizza team takes care of its franchisees also makes it personal: "To me, it's a family. I can't think of one franchisee across the country I don't get a phone call from if I'm in the area, and they say, 'Come on over for dinner'. And to me that makes all of the difference in the world".

Treliving adds: "You have to change the word *culture* to *people* because they're the ones that create this other word called *culture*. It's not me, it's not George—it's a feeling. The one word that has really made me successful is *people*. They don't work for me, they work with me. And it's a team, there's no 'I'".

Clearly an organization like Boston Pizza values its team approach, because it aligns with the company's values as an organization, and it also draws a direct line to its profitability: keeping the franchisees happy is simply good business.

Other organizations are much more individually focused and require a high contribution from individuals. This isn't at the cost of the team, but individuality is clearly more valued and rewarded.

Which behaviours are recognized and rewarded in your organization?

3. A Focus on Cost Control versus a Focus on Happy Customers

There are very few organizations that can walk the line between keeping costs down and keeping customers happy. In fact, this is where many businesses can go wrong. What we're talking about here is how concerned your top performers are with happy customers, compared with their focus on minimizing operating costs (at the expense of customer service). These competing sets of priorities can sometimes lead to mixed messages, and mixed behaviours by your leadership team. This is also why what an organization like WestJet has done is even more incredible. In a low-cost, small-margin business, it has been able to keep costs down without compromising its focus on the "guest experience".

4. A Focus on Accessibility versus a Focus on Distance

Do the leaders and/or the top performers on your leadership team feel they should keep a distance between themselves and the rest of the organization, or do these individuals believe they should make themselves accessible? The simple fact is that if those in the middle of the organization feel they can't communicate with the higher-ups, there's a power distance. Good or bad, this is part of your culture, no matter how much your organization may have trumpeted its open-door policy or its flat structure. Behavioural mapping can provide this kind of key insight.

The Importance of Behavioural Culture

The relationship between behaviour and organizational culture is undeniable—to the benefit of some, and to the detriment of others. Culture affects the organization, but the opposite is true, too—often referred to as the chicken or the egg question.

In any event, it's extremely important that you know the type of behavioural culture that exists in your organization—to find out what kind of behaviour is either making your culture work or taking it down.

We all know that behaviour is a learned habit. New employees are socialized in many ways—they see the habits of those who are successful at the organization, and if they want to be recognized and rewarded for their own success, they will mimic those behaviours. Those behaviours are a major part of the organization's culture, and they're supported and driven by the behaviour of the leader—or by the leadership.

WestJet's Ferio Pugliese probably sums it up best:

Strong, sustainable cultures are built on leadership. Which means if I'm a leader that's impassioned about culture, about employee empowerment, engagement, and transformation, I need to get that same passion in the hearts and in the minds of my leaders—whether it be a team leader or a vice president. If that isn't there, then they're the wrong guys for your operation.

The behaviour of individuals within a culture will be influenced greatly not only by the general organizational culture but also by the behaviours that are encouraged and exhibited by the higher-ups. Whatever those behaviours are, your high performers will have them. So why not go to thse individuals to get an understanding of your culture?

That's why the answer is in the stars.

Chapter 3

The Few and the Mighty: Essential Tools to Align Culture in Your Organization

---

People who work together will win, whether it be against complex football defenses, or the problems of modern society.

—Vince Lombardi

To WestJet's Clive Beddoe, saving $250 is a big deal.

It was 1999, back in the days when you could still join a captain in the cockpit, especially if you were the CEO of the airline. Beddoe, the founding shareholder and now chairman of WestJet (and a pilot himself), was sitting in the jump seat listening to the captain speak to the ground staff while they waited to take off from Calgary, en route to Vancouver.

The discussion centered on whether or not the aircraft should be tankered—meaning filled with fuel—prior to takeoff. Although there were many considerations involved in the pilot's decision, Beddoe was keen to tanker in Calgary, given that the cost of fuel was higher in Vancouver.

"The pilot's on his calculator and he's calculating wind, he's calculating weight, he's calculating weather, and I'm thinking what the hell is this guy doing", Beddoe told me during our interview in Calgary in March. "He got on the blower and said, 'We'll take just so much fuel; we won't tanker today', and I was pissed off because I knew the price of fuel differential was quite significant and certainly warranted tankering".

Because of flight deck procedure, Beddoe—fuming—had to wait until the aircraft reached 10,000 feet before he could ask the pilot about his decision.

"I said, 'Okay, can you tell me what's happening today—we're not tankering fuel?' And he said, 'No, we're not', very confidently", recalled Beddoe. "And I said, 'Why not?' And he said, 'The temperature up here today is –55, and if we tankered fuel between here and Vancouver, by the time we land, the fuel in our wings will be about –8 degrees, and when we land in Vancouver the relative humidity is 78 percent, and with the wings at that temperature, frost will form. I calculated the cost of the de-icing fluid, and we're $250 better off by not tankering fuel'".

"And I said, 'Hallelujah, brother! Give me five!' I guarantee that was the only captain anywhere in the world that did that calculation that day. And he was thrilled to have done it and he was proud as punch", said Beddoe.

Aligning Interests at WestJet

Where does that kind of employee motivation come from, especially in an industry that is well known for its labour disputes and disgruntled employees (not to mention disgruntled travellers)?

Really, what drove that WestJet pilot to go through so much to save a mere $250?

Beddoe and his partners launched WestJet in Calgary, Alberta, in 1996. Despite its humble beginnings, WestJet's goal was to be a different airline—one with a low cost structure, but also focused on customer care and on delivering a remarkable guest experience. To Beddoe, those pieces could fit together only with a strong, aligned culture. In fact, from the outset, systems were specifically put in place at WestJet to drive both the short- and long-term behaviour of its people, so that the interests of the employees would be aligned with those of the airline.

How did they do it? As we'll see, Beddoe and his partners incorporated two key programs that would become the foundation for aligning culture throughout the company: profit sharing and an employee share-purchasing plan. In other words, they used compensation—one of the "Few and the Mighty" on our list—as an alignment tool.

The Need to Align Culture

We believe that culture is the only sustainable competitive advantage an organization has; it is the only pure thing that differentiates your company, thereby driving your performance. Your competitors can adopt your strategy. They can copy your innovations if they want. They can even attempt to steal your clients or customers. But they can't duplicate your culture.

Every day, everywhere people gather for purposeful work—in corporations, in schools and universities, in associations, in foundations, and in charitable organizations—and the culture either works or it doesn't. It either enhances the organization's strategy or works against it. It's one of the two, and if you're hoping for the former (aren't we all?), aligning your culture is the only way to truly make it work for your organization. Identifying and defining culture, as we talked about in Chapter 1, and articulating culture, as we'll discuss in Chapter 5, are also critically important. But developing and aligning systems in your organization to support culture is the only true way to make it happen.

How do we know this?

Because of the high-performance organizations we've worked with through our executive search and cultural assessment practices over the past 10 years, of course. But also because of our firm's annual awards program—Canada's 10 Most Admired Corporate Cultures—which is now in its seventh year. In many ways, Canada's 10 is like our firm's R&D lab. Whether it's the thousands of leadership surveys in our Canadian Corporate Culture Study, the hundreds of yearly Canada's 10 program submissions and interviews, our annual Corporate Culture Summit, our regional events, or our national Canada's 10 gala, we've been at the forefront of best practices in culture and fit. And what our exposure to these high-performance organizations has told us is this: if your culture is aligned with your strategy and your employees are aligned with your culture, you're going to get enormous engagement, and you're going to get fantastic results. Remember what some of these results have told us, as we talked about in Chapter 1: our 2010 winners of Canada's 10 Most Admired Corporate Cultures, in terms of a three-year compound annual growth rate, outpaced the S&P/TSX 60 by an average of nearly 600 percent—or six times. This performance has been repeated year after year

Tools to Align Your Culture

- Performance management
- Leadership
- Compensation
- Recognition
- Celebration
- Training and development
- Organizational history
- Corporate social responsibility
- Organizational structure

with every new list of Canada's 10 winners: organizations with strong, aligned cultures outperform their peers.

Alignment is the key in terms of the systems required to support the culture. It's absolutely critical.

Alignment Tool 1: Performance Management

Performance management essentially involves an annual or biannual review of performance at prescribed times. The key to performance management in terms of culture alignment, however, is this: it should be as much about behaviours as it is about actual outcomes.

I'll use my daughter's mite-level softball team as an example. I'm the coach of the team, a group of about 12 eight- to ten-year-olds (and one tenacious seven-year-old). We won the other day, and afterwards I sat the team members down and told them that the only reason they had squeaked out a win was because of their athletic ability, not because they were living up to the kind of team ethic and the kind of culture that we had agreed upon as a group. You see, our girls set their own goals for the season, such as "to hit a home run and to win the championship" or "to catch better". We also agreed that we would have a culture of teamwork, of continuous improvement, of being fast and aggressive, but also one of sportsmanship and fair play.

You can imagine the looks I received in response when I questioned them on their win.

"But we won; isn't that a good thing?" they asked. And I said yes, we won, but my postgame speech was really about how they won. That part of it wasn't great. They won because of their skill, not because they had worked together as a team. In other words, they got lucky. So in the following week's practice, we focused on the behaviours we needed to modify in order to be a better team, rather than focusing only on hitting and fielding. As I write this book, our girls are 14–0 in their 22-game season. Do I link that solely to our culture? Of course not. We do have a lot of talent. But most important, we have a bunch of great kids with wonderful attitudes, with staff members and parents who are aligned with the culture. We're not likely to go 22–0, nor is that our goal. But any success we have will be due to the culture we've created, a culture that is aligned through our systems, supported by our parents, and, most important, led by our coaches and team leaders.

Mite-level girls' softball aside, however, here is the real challenge I'll issue to anyone who is running an organization: if measuring behaviours is not a component of your performance management today, it should be. If you're aligning your performance reviews with your organization's values, that's a good start, but that's not always an easy thing to do. It's difficult to catch people "living" values. Values are about how you make decisions, about what you consider important. What you really want to do is catch people engaging in the behaviours that allow them to live the values. See the difference?

Let's look at a few examples.

Acklands-Grainger Inc. Acklands-Grainger is based in Richmond Hill, Ontario, north of the city of Toronto. With 170 branches, six distribution centres, and more than 2,200 employees across Canada, it is the country's largest distributor of industrial, safety, and fastener products.[1] What does that mean? As Court Carruthers, the senior vice president of Grainger International and president of international business, including Canada, explained to our audience at our annual Corporate Culture Summit in

February: "We sell hammers and toilet paper and hard hats, to big business and government, around the world". Acklands-Grainger is also proud of the fact that it keeps its customers running safely each and every day.

Founded in Winnipeg in 1889 and incorporated as Acklands in 1904,[2] the organization grew—through both internal growth and acquisitions—to become the leader of the pack in Canada. In 1996, Acklands was purchased by Lake Forest, Illinois–based Grainger, a $7.5 billion company that had been in business for 100 years; Grainger had 18,000 team members operating in 20 different countries and was the largest industrial distributor in the United States.[3] (At the time of the purchase in 1996, the Acklands name was changed to Acklands-Grainger Inc.[4])

We will take a deeper dive into the Acklands-Grainger culture later in the book, and look at the key steps its leadership took to drive the performance of the 120-year-old organization. But for our purposes here, suffice it to say that the implementation of key operating principles at Acklands-Grainger, which then became the organization's performance drivers, was essential to driving its recent success.

Once Carruthers and his team in Canada introduced this simple, yet comprehensive set of operating principles, it became the basis of all decisions and of everything that Acklands-Grainger does as an organization.

With some slight changes, these operating principles have become performance drivers for the entire Grainger organization worldwide. And

---

Acklands-Grainger Inc.—Operating Principles

- *Customer focus.* Deliver exceptional service to targeted customers. All team members serve the customer or serve those who do.
- *People focus.* Attract, retain, and develop the right talent. Create a healthy, safe, and open environment for them to thrive.
- *Winning attitude.* Work as a team to compete hard and win.
- *Urgency and simplicity.* Do it now. Keep it simple.
- *Living the values.* Do the right thing, always.[5]

they're not just a guideline for everyday employees. Right up the organization, the operating principles play a key role in decision making.

"If I'm ever confused about a decision, I can look at this sheet of paper, I can look at my wallet card, I can look at my phone, I can look on the wall, and if I'm doing something that aligns with those five things, then I know I am making the right decision", says Carruthers.

The performance drivers are also the basis for reviews and promotions at Acklands-Grainger. In fact, the only thing that gets measured or discussed in a performance review is the five principles and the behaviours related to them. Team members receive a numerical ranking on each of the five.

Laurie Wright, the senior vice president of human resources at Acklands-Grainger, drove home this point at our Corporate Culture Summit in February of 2010: "All of our internal HR functions are very much based on the operating principles", she told our audience. "Whether it's our talent review process or our succession plan, people are measured not only on what they achieve, but it's on the 'how'. 'How' will always trump the 'what'. Whether it's hiring or assessing individual performances, it's always primarily about the 'how'".

Maple Leaf Foods   At Maple Leaf Foods, performance appraisals are based on adherence to the Leadership Edge, a series of values written by president and CEO Michael McCain that defines the kinds of behaviours the organization wants its people to hold in common, and to practice and reinforce. These include "Do What's Right" (act with integrity, behave responsibly, and treat people with respect), "Getting Things Done in a Fact-Based Disciplined Way" (seize the initiative with the highest level of urgency and energy; understand and connect with consumers and stakeholders), and "Dare to Be Transparent" (have the confidence and courage to be candid and direct, communicate openly in a trusting manner and act with passion, conviction, and personal humility).[6]

The Leadership Edge forms the basis of performance appraisals at Maple Leaf Foods. In fact, every employee at Maple Leaf Foods is ranked. The ratings aren't public, but each employee knows his overall number. The organization uses a straightforward matrix based on two key criteria to come up with the ranking: first, "results achieved", and second, "values consistency". And if there's a tie between results achieved and consistency with the behaviours outlined in the Leadership Edge? At Maple Leaf Foods, values trump results.[7]

Maple Leaf Foods is measuring behaviour, not just results, and that's a powerful way to align corporate culture with your business strategy.

Yellow Media Inc.   Yellow Media Inc., Canada's number one Internet and leading performance media and marketing solutions company, has three organizations under its umbrella—Yellow Pages Group (YPG), Trader Corporation, and Canpages—and employs 4,143 people.[8]

At Yellow Media, half of an employee's performance appraisal is based on what she accomplished in terms of results, using established metrics. The other half is based on how she did it. In other words, Yellow Media wanted to instil and align a culture in which its people were also rewarded for living the organization's stated values.

"Half our performance appraisals are the 'how'", Marc Tellier, president and CEO of YPG and CEO of both Trader and Canpages, told the audience at our Corporate Culture Summit in 2010. "Like everyone else, we have scorecards and we have metrics; that part is empirical, and it's relatively straightforward. But the other half of the performance appraisal is: how did you do it? If you pissed everyone else off while you were doing it, I'm not sure you're living the values. Don't get me wrong, we're about as performance oriented as they come. But the 'how' is as important as the 'what'. And I would argue if someone demonstrates the right qualities on the 'how', it's almost guaranteed that the 'what' is going to be there".

Agrium Inc.   Agrium is a major retail supplier of agricultural products and services in North and South America and a leading global producer and marketer of agricultural nutrients and industrial products.[9] As CEO Mike Wilson told me in April, the Calgary-based company has 12,000 employees, has a market cap of $15 billion, and has seen significant global growth in the past decade.

In size and financial scope, Agrium is a very different company from the one that Wilson joined as chief operating officer in 2000 and took over as CEO in 2002. We'll learn more about the kind of culture change that Wilson implemented at Agrium later in the book, but one of the key changes involved performance management.

"All employees were rated on a scale of 1 to 10 when I came in", Wilson told me. "The lowest anyone was rated was a 6, and the highest anyone was rated was a 9. There weren't any 3s; there weren't any 10s".

With his new senior vice president of human resources, Jim Grossett, Wilson implemented a new forced ranking system. And how was employee performance then measured, moving forward? It was based on an individual's adherence to Agrium's five-point Formula for Success. In other words, as at Maple Leaf Foods, Yellow Media, and Acklands-Grainger Inc., performance reviews at Agrium were to be based not only on what an employee accomplished (in terms of meeting goals and targets and other such measures), but also on how he accomplished it. Despite initial resistance, this approach is now understood to be a key component of Agrium's success.

"Literally to a person, almost every one of the senior folks that balked at forced ranking has, three years later, basically said, 'You know, it's one of the best things we ever did'", says Wilson.

Performance management is a key tool to help your organization, but only if it focuses on measuring behaviour (in addition to outcomes and results).

Two other quick points about performance management:

- Performance management should be informal as well as formal. The key here is to catch people exhibiting the right behaviours. It can be as simple as saying, "That was great" when the person's actions truly represented the key behaviours that your organization

Agrium Inc.—Formula for Success:

- Results orientation
- Ownership mindset
- Integrity
- Capacity for change
- Inspired leadership[10]

espouses. Or, it could be as simple as sitting down with a top performer and talking about it, as in, you've seen her exhibit a certain behaviour, and you'd like to see more of it. The key is to link informal performance management to who you are as an organization.

■ Performance management can be affected by the talent review process. Talent reviews should be collaborative and open. They should also be example-centric. If there are no examples, nothing can be challenged. And I'm not saying that all reviews should be challenged, but what you need to do is come armed with examples of things that someone has done really well. That's information that you can't make up. Because of their collaborative nature, talent reviews are a wonderful opportunity to ask *how* something was done.

Alignment Tool 2: Leadership

In our annual Canadian Corporate Culture Study, we ask respondents to identify what has led to the evolution of their organization's corporate culture. In the 2011 survey, 92 percent gave "current leadership" as their number one response to this question.

Leaders have an enormous influence on the culture of an organization. Whether it's CN's Hunter Harrison, the Princess Margaret Hospital Foundation's Paul Alofs, Yellow Media's Marc Tellier, Maple Leaf Foods' Michael McCain, or any of the other leaders we'll read about elsewhere in the book, leaders play a key role in defining and shaping culture. And the manner in which those leaders drive the communication of that culture is the key to its success. Leadership is an obvious and

	Response Percent
Current leadership	92.0%
Current employees	70.9%
Former employees	26.8%
Former leadership	34.6%
Company history	66.1%
Merger & acquisition	12.6%

Source: Waterstone Human Capital, "2011 Canadian Corporate Culture Study".

Figure 3-1   What Has Led to the Evolution of Your Current Corporate Culture?

mandatory alignment tool if an organization is to have any hope of using culture to drive its performance.

Alignment Tool 3: Compensation

I often talk to our clients about the importance of linking compensation systems to culture. I usually get a raised eyebrow or a look of confusion in return. Some will say that linking compensation to culture is impossible. Others ask: How do you do that? How do you link remuneration to who you are?

The issue I have with compensation systems is that either they're arbitrary or they're linked only to performance and outcomes. If culture is about behaviour, as we've discussed, then you've got to link a significant component of your compensation systems to behaviour—and the really innovative organizations, like those in our examples earlier in this chapter (Acklands-Grainger, Yellow Media, Agrium, and Maple Leaf Foods), have already figured out that doing so is an obvious and important tool in aligning culture.

Here's another point that I'll make up front: if your organization claims to have a performance-based culture, you need to determine what part of your compensation is effective. Historically, base compensation has been used as the major tool in performance-based compensation systems. The reality is, since inflation is so low, and given all of the fixed costs associated with base salaries, modern compensation systems should really be focusing more on variable compensation—with much of it tied to core behaviours. It's a question of making it clear to your people that base compensation is going to go up only modestly with inflation, even if they're high performers. The only time this might change is if an individual is moved into a higher position—and even then, variable compensation, not base, should be the focus. Some organizations have figured out a way, through either short-term, medium-term, or deferred long-term compensation, to make their variable compensation extremely high (tying it not just to what people achieved but to how they achieved it). And this makes the culture of these organizations much more performance-based. If your company is not doing this kind of thing, and you're saying that you have a performance-based culture, you'll have a massive problem on your hands: your culture will cease to have that aspect of being performance-based.

The perfect case study on the subject of performance-based compensation, and on the use of compensation as an alignment tool, is WestJet. Because it is such a cost-focused organization, it rewards profitability. It has figured out that part of the rewards system.

Here's how WestJet did it.

WestJet   Back in the early to mid-1990s, when Clive Beddoe and his partners were putting the pieces together to launch WestJet, they knew that things needed to be done differently. In Beddoe's view, Canada's airline industry was broken: it was inefficient, and it had an extraordinarily high cost structure. Beddoe looked outside of Canada for inspiration, and he saw Southwest Airlines as a model for a new and innovative approach.

"The key to the success of Southwest was twofold: one was its cost structure and the other was its culture", Beddoe told me. "There were some elements in the way in which Southwest operates that we can't duplicate here because our regulatory environment is different. But you could replicate much of the same sorts of things—one type of airplane, employee engagement, aligning the interests of the employees with those of the company—so we looked at how they did that. We had to take the Southwest way and 'Canadianize' it".

Beddoe and his partners incorporated two key programs that became the foundation for aligning culture throughout the company:

1. *Profit sharing.* Unlike other airlines, Southwest offered 10 percent of its profits to its employees, who in turn had the option of taking that profit and putting it into Southwest stock. Beddoe decided to take this idea one step further at WestJet.

   "If we say our employees are the most important part of our organization, then why don't we prove it by having a profit-sharing program be a function of the profit?" says Beddoe. "The more money we make, the more of that profit we give to the employees".

   What this meant for a WestJet employee was a minimum 10 percent profit share. However, the rate at which the employees participate in the profit would grow by the same rate as the profit, capped at 20 percent.

"Now there's this exponential growth that occurs", says Beddoe. "Wouldn't that overcome the sort of union mentality that invades an organization? Because the unions say, 'We're not getting our fair share', but if you actually design a structure that automatically grows the amount of profit share with the growth of the profitability of the organization, how can you say you're not getting your fair share?"

Beddoe notes that in 2000, the company had an almost 20 percent margin, and the airline's payout that year was $12,000 per employee—at a time when the average salary was $28,000.

"We set that structure up right from Day One", says Beddoe. "Get everybody engaged with the same mindset that *profitability* is a great word, not a dirty word; profitability is something we should all strive for; profitability unites us all with a common cause. So that's what we did".

2. *An employee share purchase plan.* The Employee Share Purchase Plan at WestJet bills itself as one of the most lucrative in the country. Employees can purchase up to 20 percent of their gross salary in WestJet shares, and the company will match the contribution, dollar for dollar.

"Southwest had just done profit sharing rolled into stock. I wanted profit sharing *and* stock," says Beddoe. "Profit sharing drives short-term behaviour; stock drives long-term behaviour. I didn't want one to jeopardize the other."

Beddoe's inspiration for this plan came from a colleague of his who was running an oil and gas company and offering a lucrative profit-sharing plan of 5 percent of an employee's salary. Given that salaries were much higher in the oil and gas industry than at WestJet, Beddoe decided to quadruple the percentage. In addition, there was only a one-year hold on the stock.

"In essence, that said to the employees, 'Look, buy the stock, and at the end of the year you can sell it, and if the stock hasn't fallen by 50 percent, you've made money'", says Beddoe. "But having bought stock and having got used to having put their hand in their pocket, they now start to think and behave differently—they're owners". And owners, as many of us know, behave differently.

To Beddoe, incorporating both an employee share-purchasing plan and a profit-sharing plan created an alignment between the employee and the employer—WestJet and its people—who now shared the same interests.

"By doing those two things, I think what we achieved was a behavioural change", says Beddoe. "We got the core of the culture in place by virtue of this, and then we fed it with all of the other activities—adding a vice president of culture, the profit-sharing celebrations, and so on".

From this, the now famous WestJet culture emerged.

Benefits and Nonfinancial Compensation

Aligning compensation systems should also take benefits and nonfinancial compensation into consideration.

Benefits   Historically, particularly in a country like Canada, employee benefits packages have been hierarchical and have done a better job at supporting employees as a generic, mass group. Flex-based benefits are a better choice in order to create programs that are tailored to different individuals and their needs. If you encourage a work-life balance within your organization, for instance, or you're trying to support the lives of your employees, the individual-based or flexible benefits programs can be of great value. These programs are not always feasible or affordable for small businesses, but for medium to large organizations, flex benefits are the way to go and are the better tool for supporting and aligning culture. This is especially true today, in the age of individualism and "it's about me".

Pensions are, of course, another type of benefit—both revered and envied, depending on your own situation and perspective.

One of our Canada's 10 Most Admired Corporate Cultures of 2010 was HOOPP—the Healthcare of Ontario Pension Plan—one of the largest and most successful pension plans in Canada. HOOPP provides a defined-benefit pension plan to Ontario's hospital and community-based healthcare sector. The organization invests the assets, administers the plan, and pays more than $1.2 b... benefits to more than 260,000 plan members an...

As we all know, pension shortfalls have... HOOPP's performance story is drastically diff... has to do with the culture of this organization. A... the Great Recession, the HOOPP fund had $51.1 billion ... ... available for benefits, an increase of $4.4 billion over the previous year; HOOPP was 102 percent funded at that point in time.[12] In 2010, the fund was valued at more than $35.7 billion.[13]

What's equally as remarkable about HOOPP is that it's an organization with a unified voice, expressing a single-minded purpose: delivering on the pension promise. Many people in the organization rally to this mantra, and they value the compensation derived from their own pension. They know that their pension is never going away; they know that it's significant, and it's sticky in terms of being a retention tool. It's also aligned with the culture. Could you imagine a pension organization that doesn't have a fantastic pension benefit? It's clearly a part of the culture and helps align the culture, and for many HOOPP employees, it's one of the key reasons that they're there.

Nonfinancial Compensation

1. *Travel benefits.* Take a look at an organization like WestJet. Employees receive unlimited travel. They even have the ability to issue a certain number of passes to family members every year. It's an important form of nonfinancial compensation at the airline, and equally as important, it is aligned with the culture.

2. *Special budget.* At Boston Pizza, each employee is issued a certain amount so that she can eat at other casual dining restaurants. It's a benefit that's great for employees, but it also provides the company with excellent competitive insights—it gets its people into other restaurants, not just its own.

3. *Other employee perks.* Golf tournaments and NHL games are a big part of the culture at Boston Pizza. And employees are right in there with the franchisees, taking part. For many, hosting franchisees in a private box at an NHL game or running a golf tournament in Florida

ous perk, and a great form of compensation that is completely
ned with the organization's culture. Sports and families are
revered at Boston Pizza—it's a really big part of who the company is.

4. *Bonus vacations.* At our firm, after five years of service, our people
are given a four-week bonus vacation that can be attached to their
regular vacation time. Some organizations give a six-week bonus
after ten years. In our case, the bonus time is designed to be a sab-
batical, and we believe it's the type of perk that reinforces our culture—we want to support the personal lives of our people, and we
believe that giving them this kind of personal time off helps to
accomplish that.

5. *Spot rewards.* These rewards are often based on peer or leadership
nomination. A spot reward could be a lunch, a dinner, or a gift certificate. The key is that it's recognizing someone on the spot with a
gift, or through some sort of communication or public thank you.
These should be given out to individuals as a reward for living the
culture of the organization.

All these forms of nonfinancial compensation are great, particularly
if they are aligned with your culture. Understanding which ones work,
and not just implementing these programs for the sake of having them,
is critical. In other words, whether it's a spot reward or a travel benefit,
you need to ensure that it is aligned with your culture.

Alignment Tool 4: Recognition

There are all sorts of ways to recognize people that are not compensation-
based. The question is, how many recognition programs are truly behav-
ioural-based? Linking recognition programs to behaviour is a massive
opportunity for organizations.

Here are a few examples of recognition programs that truly understand this concept:

1. *Agrium Inc.'s CFO Day.* Every June, Agrium's CFO, Bruce
Waterman, takes the Calgary corporate head office group to a ranch
in nearby Kananaskis, in the foothills of the Canadian Rockies. The

goal is a day of play. But the objective is linked to behaviours—it's to recognize and appreciate employees for their work over the past year. Agrium is pretty blunt about what it perceives to be the value of recognizing its employees. As it stated in its awards submission to our Canada's 10 Most Admired Corporate Cultures program: "Recognition plays a role in enabling Agrium to engage employees and drive behaviours and results that support the delivering on our objectives".[14] I couldn't have said it better myself!

2. *Direct Energy.* With 2,500 employees in Canada and more than 3 million customers, Direct Energy is one of North America's largest competitive energy suppliers. As an organization, it attributes its success to its values-based culture.

    Direct Energy has a very clever recognition program called Platinum Awards, an open process in which peers nominate other peers in categories that are aligned with the organization's values. Teammates are invited to "Fun Fairs" where they talk about why they won. This then culminates in a gala event, where those same employees receive cash and other prizes.[15]

3. *The Acklands-Grainger President's Club.* Every spring, top customer-facing performers at Acklands are given the opportunity to join the organization's president and executive team for an all-inclusive weeklong trip for themselves and a companion, typically to the Caribbean, Mexico, or Hawaii. The objective of the President's Club is to recognize and celebrate the success of the organization's top performers[16]—and as we know from earlier in this chapter, employees are measured based on their adherence to the principles and behaviours outlined in the Acklands' performance drivers.

4. *The Mini Cooper Program at Coastal Contacts.* Coastal Contacts is the leading online direct-to-consumer retailer of replacement contact lenses, eyeglasses, and optical products. Every quarter, the organization's top five performers are recognized by being given access to one of five Mini Coopers, which they can drive for three months. How do they earn this recognition? Employees are given stars throughout the quarter for their adherence both to core values and to key performance indicators. At the end of the quarter, the employee with the most stars wins.[17]

In any recognition program, the key is to tie the accolades to both outcomes and behaviour, in order to make recognition an effective alignment tool.

Alignment Tool 5: Celebration

Recognition can also involve celebration. Celebrations can create culture because they create shared experiences. In fact, the types of celebrations that an organization holds say a lot not only about what the company values but also about its culture. We will look at culture and celebration in detail in Chapter 7, but the point I'll make here is this: like recognition and rewards, compensation, and all of the other alignment tools, how you celebrate with your organization needs to have a point. It shouldn't just be parties for the sake of having parties. Celebrations should be aligned with who you are as an organization — and when they do that effectively, how you celebrate will help to reinforce and align your culture.

Alignment Tool 6: Training and Development

Training and development are excellent tools for aligning culture. In Chapter 6, we'll argue that training shouldn't just be skills-based. Not only will we debunk that myth, but we'll also make the case that for training to truly be used as a cultural alignment tool, organizations should be focusing on training for fit—in other words, training, reinforcing, and rewarding the key behaviours of their top performers (and, of course, of their leaders).

Alignment Tool 7: Organizational History

Reviewing and reflecting on the organization's history is also an important cultural alignment tool. The key is for an organization to make the link between the organization's past and its current culture. Furthermore, it's a real advantage on this front if an organization can really understand and clarify its fundamental reason for being. Call it a credo or a mantra — call it what you will. A good example is Shoppers Drug Mart, Canada's largest retail drug store group, which has been in business for 49 years. Its internal employment brand is "My Shoppers, More Ways to Care". Shoppers prides itself on having gained the trust of Canadians through its professional service, knowledge, and friendly advice. The organization sees "My Shoppers, More Ways to Care" as an expression of its corporate culture and as a representation of the near half-century-long commitment it has made to its customers and to its employees.[18]

Alignment Tool 8: Corporate Social Responsibility

Many organizations embark on corporate social responsibility (CSR) programs. The best ones tie those initiatives back to their culture.

TELUS is an incredible story on the CSR front. Under the guiding philosophy of "We Give Where We Live", since 2000, TELUS has contributed $245 million to charitable and not-for-profit organizations. The organization has also volunteered more than four million hours of service to local communities. For its efforts, it has received incredible recognition — TELUS was named the Most Outstanding Philanthropic Corporation in the world in 2010 by the Association of Fundraising Professionals (the first Canadian company in history to receive this recognition).[19]

What's key here is that TELUS links its CSR efforts to one of its four core values — that of spirited teamwork.

"There's nothing that better epitomizes our belief that teamwork extends from the company into the community and recognizes the symbiotic relationship between the company and its community than that level of recognition", TELUS's president and CEO Darren Entwistle told me of the Association of Fundraising Professionals award.

Another incredible example of corporate social responsibility comes from Tim Hortons, the fourth largest publicly traded quick service restaurant chain in North America based on market capitalization, and the largest in Canada.[20] Tim's is an iconic brand in Canada, known as much for having created a coffee culture as for its charitable initiatives. The Tim Horton Children's Foundation runs three core campaign programs serving economically disadvantaged children: a residential camp program, a youth leadership program, and a community partnership program. Since its founding in 1974, 130,000 children and youth have benefited from one of the six foundation camps located across North America.[21]

From their humble beginnings, the camps have truly grown. Paul House, executive chairman and interim CEO of Tim Hortons, tells me that the organization now has an annual budget of approximately $25 million and in 2010 gave away $675 million in bursaries and scholarships to kids in the leadership program. In addition, a new leadership camp is in the works for northern Manitoba.

"It's a fundamental belief in making a difference", added Tim's senior vice president of human resources, Brigid Pelino, when I met with Pelino and House in July. "The moment that it has some other purpose is the moment that it's not genuine, and that's the moment it loses its magic. And it's got a lot of magic from an employee perspective, too, when we're out recruiting".

There are so many other valuable corporate social responsibility initiatives that we could mention here—like Four Seasons Hotels & Resorts and its support of the annual Terry Fox run for cancer research (it manages one of the largest Terry Fox run sites in Ontario, at Toronto's Wilket Creek Park, and over the years this event has raised $8 million for the foundation[22]) and CIBC's Run for the Cure, which raised $33 million for the Canadian Breast Cancer Foundation in 2010.[23] What makes each of these even more successful is that the programs are aligned with the behaviours of the organization.

Alignment Tool 9: Organizational Structure

The structure of your organization affects your culture. Call it "human resources", call it "organizational development", call it what you will: this is about how leaders are organized. And how you do this can say a lot about the culture of your organization.

If you're a bureaucratic organization, one of the things I'm certain of is that you have a lot of levels. Why? Because levels protect people, and they're often part of a risk management strategy—at a bank, for instance. If you need various levels of approval, your structure is going to be much more bureaucratic. You'll have a lot more checks and balances, and consequently you'll be slower.

In my view, flatter structures support a "get it done", hands-on cul ture. In order for this to be truly effective, leaders need to be in the field— they need to get around. As we'll read in the next chapter, Hunter Harrison's leadership style at CN involved getting out of the corporate head office, visiting train yards, and holding leadership camps. He created a structure, and a culture, that allowed that to happen.

Tim Hortons is probably one of the best at applying this strategy: it is flat, with clear functional leaders (a head of HR, a head of marketing, and so on); it promotes from within; everyone is under one roof; and it is focused on supporting its franchisees and on being innovative. One of its cultural imperatives (in fact, it's one of the company's five core values) is "We Are 'Can Do'". It really is a "get it done" culture, right from their top people down. There's no "leading from Oakville" (as in Oakville, Ontario, the location of the corporate head office). The company has an office there, but decisions are made based on what happens in the field; they are operational. The "get it done" style is supported by the structure. It is very hands-on.

You'd probably never know this as a WestJet customer, but executives who fly WestJet—in fact, any WestJetter who happens to be taking a flight on the airline—stay behind to help clean the plane. I realize that this isn't a formalized organizational development strategy, but it's symbolic and it supports WestJet's low-cost structure and its hands-on culture (it also saves the airline $13 million a year[24]). It's also an expectation, and it helps reinforce WestJet's "work together" culture.

Conclusion

If an organization aligns its systems—through performance management, leadership, compensation, recognition, celebration, training and development, organizational history, organizational structure, and corporate social responsibility—the systems will align with the culture. Why? Because everything you're then doing as an organization, whether it's conscious or unconscious, will fit in with who you are.

When this happens, you're going to get a higher level of employee engagement, and self-selection might even start to occur. In fact, in any organization, if self-selection starts to happen, alignment is working.

The important thing to remember when aligning your systems with your culture, and why we've called this chapter "The Few and the Mighty", is that you need to do only a few things really well.

If you can understand your culture, act to develop your corporate and employee brand, and then create alignment around your purpose, it's very easy to build systems around who you are. Think of it in steps: identify who you are (Know Thyself), articulate that knowledge (through leadership and through conversations about your culture, two ideas that we'll address next), understand the systems, and align with them.

The final piece of advice on aligning your culture with your systems: keep it simple. Don't try to overwork it or to do everything perfectly and all at once. Make it easy and focus on the few things that are obvious.

Chapter 4

It Starts at the Top: How Leadership Impacts Corporate Culture

Example is leadership.

—ALBERT SCHWEITZER

IN 1998, ONE of E. Hunter Harrison's first challenges as the new executive vice president and chief operating officer of Canadian National Railway (now known as CN) was dealing with the permissive work practices that had developed at the railroad over time. One of these was a phenomenon known as "early quits", where staff members would work for four hours but get paid for eight.

One his second day on the job, and after spending a few hours visiting one of CN's terminals in Battle Creek, Michigan, the Tennessee-born Harrison—who became CEO of CN in 2003—discovered "early quits" in action: most of the workers had already gone home for the day.

"I said that afternoon: stop it. Stop it today, right now, all over the system—it's grounds for dismissal for any operating supervisor or officer of the company that allows this to go on", recalled Harrison. "And these people looked at me like deer with spotlights in their eyes".

After further discussions with operations management, it was suggested to Harrison that early quits could be stopped everywhere—except in Western Canada. "And they said, 'We'll do it everywhere else but there'. And I said, 'Why not there?' And they said, 'Because those cowboys will shut this railroad down'", Harrison recalled. "And I said, 'Well, start there'".

"If you're going to be a gunfighter and you want to develop a reputation quickly, go fight the fastest gun in town. Take him on and win, and guess what—that goes a long way".

Harrison told this story in June of 2010 at a breakfast event that our firm was hosting (part of a regular series of events that we offer on corporate culture). For this particular breakfast, we had asked Harrison, along with his former colleague Les Dakens (who is now the senior vice president and chief human resources officer at Maple Leaf Foods, but who was Harrison's vice president of human resources when they were both at CN; Harrison retired at the end of 2009), to talk about culture change at the railroad. After the presentation, I also had the chance to sit down with both Harrison and Dakens to talk some more about what had taken place.

CN is one of the all-time success stories of culture change. But that change was driven by Harrison, and in fact would probably never have happened if it hadn't been for his leadership. In fact, if we want to look at how leadership can be used as a tool to align culture and drive performance, CN is a textbook case.

Culture Change at CN

Former CN CEO Paul Tellier was instrumental in that success, taking CN out of government control through a privatization in 1995. In what was perhaps Tellier's most brilliant move, he purchased Illinois Central Corporation (IC); with that purchase he got Harrison, a railroader who was going to run the business for him. Harrison certainly did take things on when he came on board at CN in 1998. His style was bold, blunt, and direct. His ideas were specific, and his vision for culture change was clear. He led the organization, while at the same time creating leaders from within.

And the impact of Harrison's leadership on CN's results is remarkable.

Most of you are aware of CN's phenomenal recent history. In 1995, the company was privatized; it was sold for $2.25 billion in what at the time was the largest IPO in Canada. In early 2010, CN's market cap was an incredible $30 billion. Harrison was at Illinois Central Corporation at the time of the IPO, and was president and CEO of that organization when it was acquired by CN in 1998. Tellier wanted Harrison as part of the deal, even though Harrison had different ideas (he was planning to retire and move on after the merger). But Tellier was insistent.

"They effectively handed me the keys to the railroad. Paul said, 'I'll run the company; you run the railroad'", said Harrison. "Now when that happens to you, that inspires results. So I quickly went to work to figure out where we were and what we needed to do".

"At that time we were lacking direction", says Harrison. "We knew we wanted to be successful—wanted to make a little money, wanted to reward shareholders—but we really didn't know what we were about. So I said, let's figure that out. People want to lead things they believe in".

The company had also made $8 billion in acquisitions. Says Harrison: "We didn't only have to change internally; we were taking on six or seven different cultures and blending them with ours".

One of Harrison's first actions was to develop CN's five guiding principles. As Harrison put it to our audience, these principles became the backbone of the company and offered a "here's what we do and here's why we do it" guideline for employees.

CN's Five Guiding Principles

1. Service (do what you say you are going to do)
2. Cost control (control costs relative to revenues)
3. Asset utilization (maximize the use of assets)
4. Safety (don't get anybody hurt)
5. People (if you don't get this one right, forget the other principles, and be passionate about what you do)

By making these changes and driving the five guiding principles throughout the organization, Harrison began the evolution from "worst to first" and got CN on its way.

And what were the results?

Les Dakens explained it to us this way: in 1995, CN's operating ratio (a measurement of efficiency in the railway industry; essentially, expenses divided by revenues) was over 100 percent. Said Dakens: "With an operating ratio, the lower the number, the better. It's like golf. Hunter took this railroad from 100, which was the worst railroad in North America, to hitting a 58 in two quarters in a row. That's unheard of". This score was also 16 points ahead of the competition.

The Need for Leadership

The idea of cultural change was not initially met with enthusiasm at CN.

On one of Harrison's first days at CN, he brought about 100 of the organization's top managers and officers together to explain his concept of precision railroading—a concept that went against the traditional method of operating, which focused on getting a train from A to B. Precision railroading, on the other hand, focuses on getting a customer's *shipment* from A to B. "And guess what?" Harrison asked our audience. "I heard no amens. There was no red carpet when I got there. People were looking at the ceilings and at the floors and at the walls. I could read in their body language, 'This too shall pass; we've been through this before'".

One of Harrison's favourite quotes is by American industrialist J. Paul Getty, who said the following: in times of rapid change, experience could be your worst enemy.

"What you've experienced in the past might be what's stopping you," explains Harrison. "So how do you change? Through leadership—through strong, motivated, skilled leaders".

Harrison admitted that he doesn't think cultural change at CN would've had the staying power it did without leadership. As a self-described "agent of change" at CN, Harrison recognized the critical importance not only of the executive team, but in particular of the direct skills of CN's supervisors. He needed champions, and, as he told our audience, he did two critical things to build that bench: Hunter Camps, and what eventually became known as the Railroad MBA.

Hunter Camps Hunter Camps, which began at CN in 2003, were 2½-day off-site leadership sessions (part classroom training, part R&R) that brought together 20 to 25 first-line supervisors and middle managers.

Originally, the group came mostly from Transportation, but it soon evolved to include every function at CN.

The key to the camps was access to Harrison himself—participants listened to and interacted with the CEO, and talked about how culture change would be achieved at CN. Harrison originally focused the sessions on his precision railroading model, but he soon broadened the scope to include the five guiding principles. The focus eventually became leadership, and the importance of people who lead well.

Initially four camps were held a year; that number eventually grew to 18 annually.

The impact was felt on both sides. "Campers" learned about what was expected of them as leaders. Harrison and Dakens, who co-ran the camp, say that they gained valuable insight into CN.

"We got to see people in a different type of environment", recalled Harrison. "And we learned all kinds of things about the organization". He cites one camp in particular, where he was particularly impressed with the skill, intelligence, and business acumen of one of the railroad's IT managers. After the camp, Harrison asked the department head about this particular employee. He learned that there was no specific plan for her, beyond the fact that she would probably replace her boss once he retired—in six or seven years. Not good enough. Harrison created a new position for the manager, and through the process, he realized two things: one, CN was overlooking its own talent, and two, department heads felt that they lacked the authority to make these types of critical promotion decisions themselves.

The Railroad MBA   The other way in which Harrison built leaders at CN was through the development of a leadership training program. Harrison recalls a senior vice president with CN, in the marketing group, who was bright and who had business sense, but who didn't have a railroading background and therefore didn't fully understand the business. Once Harrison felt that there was enough bench strength to handle this person's absence, Harrison worked to develop an 18-month program to turn this individual into a better railroader.

"And the next thing I knew? It's a 'Railroad MBA'", recalled Harrison. "Other railroads were calling us and saying, 'What university are you working with for that railroad MBA program?' Well, it was CN University".

From there, other talented leaders within the organization, some of them not quite at the senior level, were identified. Again, when bench strength allowed for it, those individuals also went through a Railroad MBA to make them more knowledgeable, well-rounded "railroaders" and better leaders.

So how successful did CN become? Here's a great anecdote, which Harrison shared with us at our breakfast series, to illustrate: in early 2009, Harrison was one of only two outsiders invited to a Bill Gates think tank. For background, consider that Bill and Melinda Gates started investing in CN in 1999.

"We were visiting, and his [Bill Gates's] financial advisor said that they were up, net, since 1999, $1.7 billion I think it was, on CN stock", said Harrison. "And I was bragging about wonderful performance, and he said, 'Yes, it paid our tax bill last year' . . . which kind of puts things into perspective".

Does it ever.

"A lot of what had to happen early on was getting employees out of the crown corp [government-owned] mentality, the entitlement mentality", Dakens noted as the presentation wrapped up. "Once we did that, I think most employees—I'd say 95 percent—wanted to be able to say to their neighbour, 'I work for one of the best companies in the railroad industry'. No, not 'one of' the best companies, *the* best company in the industry".

The Princess Margaret Hospital Foundation

I first met Paul Alofs, the president and CEO of the Princess Margaret Hospital Foundation (PMHF), in 2009. Paul had been a participant at some of our breakfast series events, and in 2010 his organization put together a submission to our Canada's 10 Most Admired Corporate Cultures program. And that year, his organization won.

This will come as no surprise if you know anything about this Toronto-based foundation. Annually, it raises $70 million in support of the Princess Margaret, Canada's leading cancer research hospital, now known as one of the top five cancer research centres in the world. It's an incredible feat, considering that the foundation manages to accomplish this from one office in Toronto with 54 employees (it raises an incredible $1.3 million per employee). In fact, it raises the second most funds of any cancer fund-raising organization in Canada.[1]

But the Princess Margaret Hospital Foundation wasn't always such a fund-raising powerhouse. It was performing, yes, but it wasn't until 2003, when Paul Alofs joined it as president and CEO, that it truly took off. It was Alofs's vision for the organization, combined with the very specific strategies that he implemented, that turned the Princess Margaret Hospital Foundation into the high-performance culture it is today.

Alofs and Culture Change

"To become a true high performance team—to be truly outstanding— it takes years", says Alofs. "We make each other better, and that's what a winning culture is all about. You celebrate the other guy's success. There's almost something magical that happens when the culture really starts working".

Alofs tells me this as we're sitting together in his office, which has a sweeping view of Queen's Park (Ontario's legislative building) and "hospital row" on University Avenue, in downtown Toronto.

I knew that Alofs, like Hunter Harrison, would be a great subject to interview for this book because of the clear line that you can draw from when he came on board at the Princess Margaret Hospital Foundation, to the tactics that he used to build and align culture at the PMHF, to the performance of the organization. The empirical evidence is clear: in 2003, when Alofs joined the PMHF, the foundation was raising $33 million a year. Seven years later, it now raises more than $70 million annually ($450 million over the last seven years). The foundation is also considered to be one of North America's most successful social enterprises as measured by effectiveness and efficiency.[2]

I'll get into an explanation of exactly what that means as we talk about Alofs and the story of how he developed a high-performance culture at the PMHF. But in Alofs's case, it's important to note that his ability to improve the culture and the performance of the organization was not based just on his knowledge, skill, and experience and on the behaviours he emulated as the president and CEO. It was also very personally motivated.

Alofs's Route to the Princess Margaret Hospital Foundation

Alofs moved back to Toronto from the United States in 2000, hot on the heels of a decade of successful, impressive career moves. In 1989, at the age of 33, he became the president of HMV Canada, growing the business from $30 million to more than $200 million in annual revenue. In 1996, he moved to BMG Music Canada, also as president (and through his efforts was named Music Industry Executive of the Year, also in 1996). After relocating to Los Angeles, Alofs then became the executive vice president and general manager of the Disney Stores of North America in 1997. He also helped launch one of the more successful IPOs of the Internet age when he took on the role of president of strategic business units for MP3.com in 1999.

But after selling his MP3.com shares (as he told me, "I got my dot.com lottery ticket punched") and heading back to Toronto, Alofs faced what he describes as a life-changing experience. His mother had had breast cancer, and it returned — with a vengeance — in 2002.

"She was the strength that brought our family together, and she asked us to look after her at home because she didn't want to be in the hospital", says Alofs, who spent most of his time with his mother in her final days, at her house in Alofs's hometown of Windsor, Ontario. "It was just the hardest thing. I literally couldn't believe how hard it was to watch someone die of cancer, someone that you care that much about. It changed me forever".

When Alofs returned to Toronto from Windsor, he shared his story with his neighbour across the street, John MacNaughton — who happened to be chairman of the Princess Margaret Hospital Foundation at the time.

"John talked to me about coming in to be president, and I thought I would do the job for two years, almost as community service", says Alofs. "But that was seven years ago. In many ways, this has been the best job I've ever had".

I'm telling you Alofs's personal story to emphasize how a leader's values can influence organizational culture. In fact, I think there are three reasons why he succeeded in creating a performance culture at the Princess Margaret Hospital Foundation: first, because of his professional experience (his impressive career in the private sector, building tier-one leadership teams); second, because of his motivation (his personal family cancer story); and, third, because of the innovative ideas he introduced (which took the form of the social enterprise model, which we will discuss next).

The Social Enterprise Model

Alofs is the first to admit that the Princess Margaret Hospital Foundation did not invent the concept of social enterprise, but he does believe that it is a leading practitioner—particularly in Canada. He also believes that the social enterprise model can be instrumental in building a transformational corporate culture within not-for-profit organizations.

So what is social enterprise?

According to Alofs, social enterprise is essentially a hybrid of the best practices from both the private sector and the not-for-profit sector.

Alofs started reading and learning about the social enterprise model while he was working in southern California in the late 1990s and while he was on the board of Covenant House. He also studied the model more formally during a weeklong course at Harvard Business School.

"Not-for-profits need to be run more like businesses," says Alofs. "And not-for-profits are so important that if we don't run them like businesses, we're going to miss huge opportunities."

According to Alofs, there are more than two million people employed in the not-for-profit sector in Canada, more than in the oil and gas industry. In addition, there are approximately 161,000 nonprofits and charities in Canada, representing $79 billion, or 7.8 percent of our GDP, making the sector larger than the automotive or manufacturing sector.[3]

"The sector is enormous in Canada and is an employer of importance", says Alofs. "Social enterprise is really about running a cause like a business, with the profit going to your cause, as opposed to shareholders".

When Alofs started at the Princess Margaret Hospital Foundation, he approached the board members about bringing the social enterprise model to the organization.

"They allowed me to bring those private-sector practices into the not-for-profit world", says Alofs. "But after a couple of years, what I realized is that the for-profit sector can learn almost as much from the not-for-profit sector in terms of the passion of volunteers, commitment, and brand building".

Alofs developed and applied three elements of the social enterprise model to the Princess Margaret Hospital Foundation: creed, inspiration, and commitment.[4] He feels that in many ways, these are like lessons, and that they can be applied to any organization—in the private or the not-for-profit world—that is interested in building a performance-based transformational culture.

Creed   "We are conquering cancer at Canada's cancer research hospital, The Princess Margaret. In our Lifetime."

This is the creed of the PMHF, developed under Alofs's leadership. To Alofs, a creed is an incredibly valuable asset, and it's what culture should be built on. We'll learn more about the power of creeds and credos in aligning culture in Chapter 8.

Inspiration   The second lesson from the social enterprise model is that of inspiration. Obviously, the foundation relies on a huge network of volunteers who are responsible for the success of the Princess Margaret Hospital Foundation's signature fund-raising events, which include Weekend to End Women's Cancers, Ride to Conquer Cancer, and Road Hockey to Conquer Cancer.

"I have people who say to me, 'The best part of my workweek is working for free'", says Alofs. "What can businesses learn from that? It's remarkable".

Alofs and his colleagues at the foundation believe that for-profit organizations can also learn to tap into the personal connections that their people have—because doing so leads to passion, and passion leads to a genuine commitment.

How is that transferable to the for-profit world?

"Think about the commitment of a volunteer. How do you find that in your own culture? I think the best private-sector companies find that and find a way to tap into it", says Alofs.

Commitment The Weekend to End Women's Cancers, now in its ninth year, asks a great deal of its volunteers: train to walk 60 kilometres in one weekend, and raise $2,000 in order to be eligible to participate. Talk about demanding a commitment.

But it works: since the event was founded, 96,000 people have done what's asked of them to participate in this event. In fact, the Weekend to End Women's Cancers has raised $285 million and, according to Alofs and his colleagues, has transformed the treatment of women's cancers in Canada. Through the funds raised, the foundation has been able to open up the Gattuso Rapid Diagnostic Centre, which provides women and men with a breast cancer diagnosis in one day, instead of weeks or months.

Demanding a commitment from volunteers is a key strategy for the foundation's signature events—and to Alofs, there's a strong example here to pass along to the private sector: that is, the importance of engaging your organization and everyone in it.

Leadership Horsepower When Alofs first came on board at the Princess Margaret Hospital Foundation, his social enterprise model wasn't necessarily greeted with enthusiasm by everyone at the foundation.

Alofs says that selling the concept of social enterprise was a process of turning the sceptics into cheerleaders. In some cases, he also had to cut his losses and move on.

"There were the people who said, 'I grew up in a not-for-profit world, and this is the way it should be running—I'm not going to listen to this'. So a couple of people left, and they had to leave", says Alofs. "And then there were the people who had a lot of questions because it seemed like a takeover by the private sector. Then they saw that it actually worked. With good leadership, if you turn the sceptics around, they can be phenomenally valuable".

To Alofs, the key to making social enterprise fly at the foundation was to bring in a top-notch leadership team.

"We were pretty unidimensional in terms of our strategies, and we had lots of good young people in development", says Alofs of his early days with the foundation. "The thing is, with culture, you can hope to do things, but if you don't have the leadership horsepower, you're never going to be able to build the kind of culture that you want."

For Alofs, this meant finding the best of the best—and that meant bringing in senior people with MBA backgrounds from the Schulich School of Business and from Harvard, and with professional experience as varied as Procter & Gamble and the United Way. Alofs says that the foundation also now has one of the best CFOs in the not-for-profit world.

And the result of his efforts?

"This is a culture of quality people", says Alofs. "You're working with people who are incredibly intelligent and educated, and almost every single person is so compassionate and caring about what they do. Bringing the social enterprise model is something that has attracted very good, like-minded people who work here, and we've had very little turnover in the last five years".

A Bold Vision: Conquer Cancer in Our Lifetime

What's so striking about the Princess Margaret Hospital Foundation is indeed its boldness. To state bluntly that the foundation is going to "conquer cancer in our lifetime" is courageous, to say the least. But it's exactly the kind of vision that's needed to tackle the magnitude of the problem—and for Alofs and his team, that bold vision had to be backed up by a drive to not only raise more money than ever before but also build the foundation's brand.

"You can come in and say you're going to increase things 5 or 10 percent", says Alofs. "But what about doubling? We were going to double the fund-raising and build a great brand. It gets people excited when you say: 'Let's double the size of this place. Let's build one of Canada's greatest brands. Let's be one of the best social enterprises in North America'".

"Conquering cancer is the basis of our culture, the basis of our brand, and the basis of our success".

It's hard to argue with the foundation's success—cancer is far from being beaten, but the Princess Margaret Hospital Foundation keeps hitting milestones. Whether it's the new Gattuso Rapid Diagnostic Centre, or the fact that Princess Margaret now has a global reputation as one of the top five cancer research hospitals, or the enormous success of the foundation's annual events, one has to wonder: would the level of success have been the same without the kind of vision, leadership, and culture that now exists at the foundation?

And would there have been as much success without Alofs's personal values and motivation?

"The chance to do something this big, to take on something this big—cancer—at a place that is one of the top five in the world in terms of research—we're in the game here in terms of being a true game changer", says Alofs. "It's unbelievably energizing and exciting every single day. It's also gut-wrenching to work here because you see so many people dying. It's an emotional place where the opportunity to do something of great importance comes together with some really talented people".

Conclusion

Paul Alofs—like Hunter Harrison was at CN—is the kind of leader whose behaviours drive the culture of the organization and therefore drive results. CN and the Princess Margaret Hospital Foundation couldn't be more different as organizations. But the strategies that their respective leaders have applied to tackle culture and turn it into a tactical and competitive advantage have definite similarities—ones that we can all learn from.

Chapter 5

The Culture Conversation: Why the Best Organizations Are Great at Articulating Their Culture

---

The single biggest problem in communication
is the illusion that it has taken place.

—GEORGE BERNARD SHAW

ONCE A WEEK, Michael McCain, president and CEO of Maple Leaf Foods, sends his weekly e-mail to each of the organization's 21,000 employees. These notes are essentially a candid review of McCain's weekly experiences and impressions: he talks about the company's activities, about success stories, and about other industry-related bits of news.[1] The main point of these notes, however, is that the examples he gives and the stories he talks about are meant to reinforce the values of the organization. It's a popular read, and it often results in one-on-one interaction between those who are reading it and the CEO.

"Every Friday, Michael talks about what he did for the week", Maple Leaf Foods' retired chief human resources officer Wayne Johnson told me. "And if you read the notes, a lot of it is, 'I did A, B, C, and D'. But what's really important is that he's linking everything he does to the values, underscoring just how important the values are".

Johnson admits that the idea was borrowed from Jacques Nassar, the former CEO of Ford Motor Co., who used to write a note to all of the employees at Ford.

"It was basically in the form of a diary: 'Here's what I did this week'", said Johnson. "Nassar would say things like, 'Monday morning I met with a couple of suppliers and I wanted to let you know that there are lots of people that want to supply Ford'. So he gave the message by diary, but also linked things to Ford's values. So Michael picked it up, and to this day has continued it".

And what are those values that McCain looks to reinforce in his weekly message? As we've discussed, Maple Leaf Foods—indeed, McCain himself—developed the organization's values under what's called the Leadership Edge. The 21 values were refreshed, relaunched, and synthesized into six in 2010. The basic premises, however, are still the same, with values including "Do What's Right" and "Get Things Done in a Fact-Based, Disciplined Way".

McCain's weekly e-mail is but one example of the way in which communication is used to reinforce the organization's culture—whether it's the *Maple Leaf Food Report* (a regular employee newsletter that gives employees updates on the Leadership Edge), town hall meetings (which are designed to reinforce the company's values and provide dialogue between management and employees), or Maple Leaf Foods' Leadership Academy, which we will talk more about in Chapter 6, the key for each of these events is that communication is the tool that is used to reinforce values and behaviour. The other important factor? These communication initiatives are leadership-driven—and in the case

---

Maple Leaf Foods—Leadership Edge Values

- Do what's right
- Deliver winning results
- Build collaborative teams
- Get things done in a fact-based, disciplined way
- Learn and grow, inwardly and outwardly
- Dare to be transparent[2]

of Maple Leaf Foods, the person who is typically in the driver's seat is the president and CEO.

Communicate Your Culture

If you believe (as we do) that culture is one of the greatest assets that an organization can have—and one that impacts performance—then it makes sense that you would want to cultivate that asset. You would want to ensure that it appreciates in value. Taking it a step further, if culture were a pure financial asset, it certainly wouldn't be left untouched on the balance sheet. Organizations would invest in it. They'd invest it in capital upgrades, in preferred stocks and bonds, and other such areas to ensure a return, so that the money didn't just sit there.

In short, they would work that asset. In fact, that's what you need to do with culture. One of the best ways to ensure that it lives, grows, and appreciates is through communication.

But that's easier said than done for many organizations.

When we started working in and around corporate culture, the word *amorphous* was used a lot. Our clients were saying to us: culture is difficult to understand, and it's hard to put any shape to it. So how can you communicate it? We don't believe that culture is amorphous. If there's no shape to the culture at a particular organization, it's because that organization hasn't yet gone through the exercise of defining it. The organization hasn't yet determined the core behaviours that both represent and drive its culture.

Once your organization has defined its culture (and we talked about how you can do this in Chapter 1), the next step is to determine how that culture will take shape so that you can articulate it.

What strategies are organizations currently using to align their culture? The results from our 2011 Canadian Corporate Culture Study show that communication is the number one tool (see Figure 5-1).

We've been told that one of the strengths of our firm is our ability to define and articulate the culture of our clients. I think the reason we've been successful at doing so is because we'll define an organization's culture in plain language that describes behaviour; for example, if the peo-

		Response Percent
Performance reviews		73.3%
Engagement surveys		63.3%
Online tools (e.g., employee blogs, newsletters, intranet)		55%
Events (e.g., leadership camps, town hall meetings)		82.5%
Leadership practices		61.7%
Training and development		73.3%
Recruitment		62.5%
Financial rewards		40.8%
Nonfinancial rewards		44.2%
Internal culture seminars		20.8%
Communication of values		84.2%
Cultural assessment		18.3%

Source: Waterstone Human Capital, "2011 Canadian Corporate Culture Study".

Figure 5-1 What Specific Strategies or Tools Are You Currently Using to Align Corporate Culture?

ple in a company behave independently, we'll say that your organization exhibits the behaviour of independence. If the people are very codependent and require a lot of cooperation, we'll use those terms, and we'll give examples to back them up.

Articulating your culture may be a challenging process, but once you get it, you need to communicate it—a lot. This can take the form of mantras, credos, rallying cries—whatever you want to call it. Sometimes the organization's mission can represent the culture (and sometimes not), but these things all help. The key is this: when you really have the ability to communicate your culture in everything you do, and when that communication comes from the top of your organization, it becomes pervasive—people truly understand what defines it. This can be from an internal/employee perspective, but also externally, to help reinforce your brand.

Great organizations communicate their culture well because they keep the message simple. For instance, look at Four Seasons Hotels and Resorts and its guiding principle of the Golden Rule (which we read about in Chapter 1). The beauty of the Golden Rule is its simplicity— it's easy to communicate, easy to understand, and easy to use as a guide

How to Communicate Your Culture Effectively

- Understand your culture.
- Keep the message simple.
- Deliver it from the top.
- Reinforce it through repetition—keep talking about it.
- Link it to your employee or consumer brands, to your systems, and to your company's history.
- Measure it against behaviour.

for behaviour. Employees can always ask themselves, am I following the Golden Rule? Am I treating people the way I would wish to be treated?

"The Golden Rule started because we wanted to reinforce the notion that a customer focus could not survive independent of an employee—the two had to work in tandem", Kathleen Taylor, Four Seasons' president and chief executive officer, told me. "In fact, employees' attitudes were mostly going to be driven by management's attitudes, and therefore how did that cycle of caring and giving flow down the waterfall from management to the employee and out to the guest".

What's also key in communicating your culture? Repetition. This means, find as many opportunities as you can to reinforce your message.

"At WestJet, we try to find as many possible opportunities as we can to just sit down and dialogue around the importance of culture", says WestJet's Ferio Pugliese. "Culture is not a bad word. It's not an airy-fairy nebulous concept. It's a true, hard value; it's a true, hard business outcome; it's a true, hard capability that people understand. And by talking about it, you're reinforcing and you're validating the behaviours that people take on day-in and day-out, and through that validation they'll repeat those behaviours".

As Pugliese told me, that's WestJet founding shareholder and chairman Clive Beddoe's simple psychology: talk to your people about how important it is to do what they do, and they'll keep doing it. Of course, that's easier to do when you have 220 employees, as WestJet did when it first started flying in 1996, rather than the almost 8,000 employees that it has today. But in Pugliese's mind, all that means is that you have to create more opportunities to communicate culture. It's as simple as that.

And how does the company do that? WestJet's culture is communicated from the top through a very simple message: Owners Care. It's a culture that's focused on caring for guests and providing a world-class guest experience. From there, the company believes that this culture, based on this simple premise, needs to be talked about—and it does so in a multitude of ways, through both its marketing communications and its employee communications vehicles.

It does it through ongoing Culture Connections, which we discussed in an earlier chapter: quarterly sessions where WestJetters and the organization's executives get together to reconnect, to discuss the latest business updates, and to share stories of their daily experiences—all done in the name of reinforcing culture.

Owners Care is such a simple, brilliant concept, but it's rooted in very specific tactics. It's aligned through the employee profit-sharing and share-purchasing plans, and that's the key. WestJetters act differently—whether they are booking flights, dealing with customers in-flight, or helping to find lost luggage—because they are owners. They literally have a stake in the business. If you then reinforce that cultural philosophy through communication and ongoing discussion on a regular basis, it becomes a part of the personal belief system of the people who work for the airline. It's in effect an employee brand. Sit in a room full of hundreds of WestJetters, as I have at one of the company's recent Culture Connection sessions, and you'll find out pretty quickly that "Owners Care" is not a forced sentiment—they've all drunk the Kool-Aid.

Leaders Must Communicate the Culture

How you articulate your culture is important, but it's really important that the leaders communicate it. If they can do it well, and if it can be done through an employee brand (or a consumer brand, if you have one), it will really help to reinforce your culture.

At our firm, for instance, our hiring credo is, "Humble, Hungry and Smart": we want to ensure that we hire people who have their egos in check, who are really motivated to be the best in their field, and who are really bright people who can counsel our clients. Our hiring credo is an important part of who we are. Not only that, but it's a credo that fits with our entire brand—and that's an important part of communicating our culture.

Let's look at Coastal Contacts, based in Vancouver. Coastal is one of the fastest-growing online retailers of contact lenses and eyeglasses, and as an organization, it prides itself on supplying its customers with the same designer brands and products that they would find in a traditional brick-and-mortar store, but for half the price. Coastal really does have a culture of low ego. But more important, its culture is built on accessibility to the people who work there.

Because Coastal is an online retailer—or e-tailer, for the sake of our discussion here—customers don't always get to meet the person who is handling their order. As an organization, Coastal has had to figure out how it's going to communicate its culture and its brand—how the company is going to show its customers who it is and what it does. It's something that Coastal has to do constantly, and often social media are heavily involved in the process.

For instance, the company has dozens of videos posted on YouTube, featuring everything from a lip dub involving hundreds of its employees from all aspects of the business (from sales to manufacturing to shipping) lip synching and dancing—complete with feather boas, balloons, and sumo wrestlers—to more information-driven videos in which Coastal's own people show off the latest frames or talk about how to order online.[3] In the case of the lip dub, part of the message was about the organization's leading corporate social responsibility initiative, the Change the View Project, whereby Coastal provides eyeglasses to people around the world who are unable to get them by their own means. The larger takeaway from the lip dub was about seeing the process—consumers and suppliers were being provided with access to the company and being shown what happens from the moment an order is placed online straight through to shipping. It's a super example of using social media to your advantage.

"There are so many components to the Coastal life right now—it's dynamic and interesting", the organization's CEO, Roger Hardy, told me.

"Our workforce has more than doubled in the past year, and there are a lot of new faces. We wanted to kind of indoctrinate those new people into what our culture is about and to show them some of the things we're doing. That was just one component".

The point is this: Coastal is constantly communicating its culture, showing who it is, what it does, and how it behaves: it's fun and it's exciting, but at the same time these communication tactics show the world what Coastal does and give people—customers—access to the organization. Currently, Coastal is hiring about 60 people a month, and its turnover rate is still below 5 percent. It's incredible what the company has been able to do. And why has it been successful? Because people have an expectation of what it's about; like WestJet's, its brand is about exceptional customer service for a low price. That's Coastal's culture, and it's communicated over and over in that way.

"What we're trying to do is to make sure the core things we're trying to deliver—speed, value, service—all those touch points are aligned with who we are, and we try to make sure the people we're hiring embody the core values we think are important", says Hardy. "But you know the culture polices itself—it's deciding if people fit or don't fit—and that's translated into how customers feel served. Hopefully when they're calling, they're dealing with someone who's engaged, who's hard-working, who really wants to make sure that their experience with our company is a 'wow' and it's a type of experience that they'll share with friends. People are passionate about what we're doing, and that's coming through at the service level".

Link to Company History

Another great way to communicate your culture and make it stick is to draw a link to the history of the company. That's not so easy to do with younger companies, like Coastal Contacts, which is now in its eleventh year of business, and WestJet, which is in its fifteenth. But long-standing companies like Johnson & Johnson, for instance, can connect how people behave with the organization's somewhat famous "Our Credo," which was crafted by Robert Wood Johnson, a former chairman of the company, in 1943. The credo essentially outlines how Johnson & Johnson will treat its employees, its shareholders, its customers, and the communities in which they live. In short, through the credo, employees get a real sense of the organization's history and thereby its culture; there is a sense of belonging to something bigger. People like to know where they've come from and why the culture is what it is. The link to history can have a significant impact on the culture of the organization. And when those two things are not in alignment, a disconnection often occurs.

Another great and more recent example is "The Schlegel Organizational Culture", an eight-page document that outlines the vision, family history, shared cultural values, and expected behaviours of Schlegel Villages, 11 continuum-of-care campuses located in southwestern Ontario and owned and managed by the Schlegel family of Kitchener, Ontario. The villages are incredibly innovative and are currently home to about 2,500 seniors, with 2,500 staff members. It's expected both of these numbers will double in the next 10 years.[4]

The document talks about how the Schlegels, beginning with company founder Ron Schlegel, have been involved in senior care since 1953 and demonstrates their very personal and unique perspective on long-term care and retirement living. It weaves this historical information into the modern-day situation and talks about the continuing role of the Schlegel family in the organization, how the business has grown, and, more important, how the Schlegels define the organization's culture.

I think every organization should go through the type of exercise required to produce this type of document. It's an excellent tool to help communicate your culture, and if the document is well written, it can be used to educate both new and existing employees. "The Schlegel Organizational Culture" document is an immediate check on "here's where we were, and here's where we are now", and it does a great job of articulating the organization's behaviours, why they're important, and how they link to the Schlegels' history and vision.

Very few organizations create this type of "Our Company's Culture" or "Our Way" document, but more should. It's one of the best recent tools I've seen, and I was very impressed. If you're an organization and you see culture as an asset, I would recommend creating a similar document.

Make It Measurable

Finally, organizations will have better luck communicating their culture when what they are communicating is something that's measurable. Often organizations are desperate to communicate their values. But values don't necessarily match the way people act, and trying to measure or talk about values the same way you do for behaviours is not easy. For instance, if integrity is one of your core values at your organization, how do you measure it? If someone has stolen or lied, it's perhaps doable, but otherwise it's hard to measure integrity on a day-to-day basis. Conversely, look at "the Golden Rule" or "Owners Care". Isn't it much easier to measure how your employees are caring, or how they're treating others? "The Golden Rule" and "Owners Care" define the organization's culture, they're easy to communicate, and they're measurable behaviours.

I'm very proud of my three daughters, Jaiden, Corsen, and Kaelen; they mean everything to me. Although I'm thrilled when someone says that they've done exceptionally well in school or in their extracurricular activities like music and sports, it's when I'm told that they are good-tempered, well-mannered, independent kids who espouse the same values even when they're not together or with their parents that I really feel proud. Why am I most proud of this? Although their mother and I are no longer together and are raising our daughters in two different homes, we've always taught a simple rule—in fact, it's the same one used at the Four Seasons: treat others as you would like to be treated. We do our best to provide our daughters with a sense of love, family, and opportunity. We have high expectations, but we'll accept failure. Why? Because it leads to success, and learning through failure helps kids be happy, healthy, and independent. We've created this culture, and I'm proud of the fact that we've done it in two different locations, if you will. Like the companies I've referred to previously, our communication of that culture has been consistent and reinforced daily.

One of my early bosses at Johnson & Johnson (J&J) was Gary Hough. Hough was a wonderful leader from J&J's pharmaceutical arm, Janssen-Ortho Inc., and he was the sales manager for the Great Lakes division of the Ortho side of the business. No one ever promoted more people (whom he and everyone else referred to as "the Lakers") into management roles than Hough. I also believe that no one understood culture like Hough. He was a communicator, a great storyteller, and a deeply caring leader, and he knew how to bring a team together through shared values, great parties, and wonderful mentoring. During one of our many discussions, Hough passed along a great piece of advice: anything important needs to be discussed, openly and honestly—whether it's a relationship, an asset, or a goal. Culture is something that must be communicated in that way. Culture conversations have to be ongoing. If culture is to be developed, honed, and valued, it needs to be communicated, it needs to be challenged, and it needs to be lived in the organization—starting at the top.

Hough was my first real boss, and he truly understood the value of culture. He hired for fit for his "Lakers", but on top of this, he worked closely with people and further reinforced the behaviour that he expected of them. As he said to me, "I can help make a diamond shine". And he did so many times over.

Chapter 6

The Train Drain

To know what people really think,

pay regard to what they do,

rather than what they say.

—RENÉ DESCARTES

FIVE WEEKS BEFORE the 1994 Winter Olympic Games in Lillehammer, Norway, speed skater Johann Olav Koss had the worst race of his life. As a native Norwegian, a world record holder, and already an Olympian in the sport, the pressure on him to perform was particularly intense.

"The papers said, 'Koss, to hell with him—he's not going to do it'", Koss told me as we sat in his office in downtown Toronto in June. Koss is the president and CEO of Right to Play, a leading international humanitarian and development organization, founded by Koss in 2001, that uses the power of sport and play to build essential skills in children who have been affected by war, poverty, and disease.[1] "I came off the ice feeling horrible, thinking, 'I have five weeks to the Olympics, and I'm not going to get there'".

Following the disastrous race, Koss asked his coach to tell him not what he was doing wrong, but what he was doing right. His objective became to focus on those four or five things, so that he could have some hope of improving in time for Lillehammer. But on the ice, Koss had to change the way he was doing things so that he used the proper technique his coach was encouraging. And it felt incredibly awkward to do so.

"My coach would say to me, if you want to be the best, you have to move your legs like this, and I would come off the ice and say, 'What are you talking about? It feels so unnatural; this is horrible'. But then I trusted the knowledge, and then I understood that I wouldn't feel natural about it. So when I felt wrong, I knew it was right".

He adds: "If you're going to change behaviour in sport, it feels extremely unnatural. But that doesn't mean it's wrong. Because that's the most effective way to win. That's actually the behaviour you have to do if you're going to win. To be efficient on the ice, or to throw the ball fast enough, you have to change behaviour to win".

Koss won three gold medals in men's speed skating in Lillehammer.

Training Behaviour

We often hear this from our clients: we can train skills, but we can't train for fit. This is a familiar refrain. We even hear it from organizations that are the best of the best in terms of aligning their culture and using their culture to drive success.

But the idea that you can train skills but not behaviour is simply not true. If it were true, none of us would be very good at child rearing, or at training pets. In fact, if it were impossible to teach behaviour, the whole idea of leadership development and organizational psychology would fall apart. (Johnson & Johnson's Gary Hough knew this long ago.)

We've talked about the importance of knowing how your high performers behave and of hiring individuals who exhibit those same behaviours. But that's only half the battle; it's not where it ends. Once those individuals have been hired, and aided by common practices like integration and the like, it is simply assumed that they will be successful. In fact, in 2011, 30 percent of the respondents to our Canadian Corporate Culture Study indicated that they had an integration process for their new leaders that lasted 90 days or less.[2] That's simply not enough time to reinforce behaviours. Even when you've recruited someone based on fit, and you assume that his behaviours are aligned with yours, the idea that the only other training you can do from that point forward is skills-based is nonsense.

Behaviour needs to be reinforced, to become unconscious and stronger. It needs to be trained and developed.

Training the Brain

First, a bit of theory: among the most significant developments in modern science in the last century is the recognition that specific aspects of human behaviour and experience are actually functions of a material structure, the nervous system. In other words, our nervous system can be trained. Now, I am not a medical doctor, nor do I have a scientific background. But as a student of organizational psychology and a former athlete, I believe this to be true: nothing affects behaviour directly except for the brain. And this is because we've allowed the environment—everything around us—to affect our brains.

If you don't believe that, ask yourself this question: have I ever been in a situation where my behaviour has changed as a result of something that is happening in my environment? I think we have all had examples of this—in either the toughest-of-the-tough or the best-of-the-best experiences.

We can train our brain to help us behave in a certain way. In executing a task, for instance, this is how it happens.

Our brain first breaks the task down into its component parts, with each part being stored in our brain. Loosely speaking, the parts are associated with each other by a line of neurons, which are strung together to form a neural pathway. Repetition is the mother of skill. Have we not all heard this before? I can't count how many times coaches have said this to me. I use that expression now when I'm coaching kids. I even say it to business leaders. It means that we learn through repetition—our neural pathway grows larger and stronger as nearby neurons are recruited to learn how to perform the task. In other words, we learn, or train ourselves and our brains, to behave a certain way if we repeat the behaviour. That's how we learn languages in the cognitive part of our brain, and it's how we learn behaviour. Isn't language effectively a behaviour—a way to teach our brain to understand and to articulate that understanding?

Now as you repeat and practice the tasks, or these connections through the central core of your brain, the behaviour gets stronger and the nearby neurons return to their previous state. In other words, they go back to where they were. But as we physically perform the activity, the movements required to begin the action become encoded in the brain's motor context, moving from neural context to action. Sport psychologists refer to this process as *muscle memory*. Again, I can remember for years and years being told by my coaches, "You've got to get it into the muscle memory". Only eventually, since I'm not the smartest guy, did I figure out that my body has to become accustomed to a certain activity—like turning, or running in a certain pattern—so that I can do it upon command. When I used to hear "quick trips right 99 alley" (which I heard a thousand times as a receiver with the Gryphons, the University of Guelph's varsity football team), my muscle memory kicked in. I knew exactly what my body was going to do and how it was going to react.

Continuing with the sports analogy, we know that the ability to perform a specific movement, such as catching a ball, without conscious thought happens as a result of the muscle memory or motor context: movements become encoded in the brain's motor context. This means that the more you practice the task, the stronger the neural path for your muscle memory becomes and the greater your ability to perform these motions using the nonconscious part of your brain becomes.

So how does this translate to leadership?

As when training athletes, we have to start with a trainable subject. If your new leader has been hired for fit, presumably she already possesses the four or five key behaviours that define success in your organization. She's what I'd call a terrific business athlete in the making. She has the athleticism and the coachable brain, and she is a proven winner. From here, and as with a sports athlete, can we not train that neural pathway and the motor context to further reinforce those key behaviours in your new hire? In other words, why can't we further train behaviour so that it continues to best represent the way a particular organization does things?

We believe this is doable. So how do you start?

Essentially, leaders need to communicate the expectation, and they then need to recognize and reward great behaviour. You won't train an athlete by reprimanding him. Negative reinforcement simply doesn't work. What does work is constant communication—the repetition of what's expected—married with positive reinforcement.

Koss concurs: "The realization of a much higher level of consciousness about what type of behaviour you want from people, because that's a type of behaviour you like to be around, becomes critical, and that needs to then be reinforced in the organization through behaviour and through recognition. That needs to be done on a very regular basis. Because again, it's the same thing as an athlete trying to train towards a world championship. Speed skating is a classic example. It's a sport where you have a very repetitive type of behaviour. Because what you're doing is technical, it's very difficult. So the movements have to be automatic. And you only create automatic behaviour through repetition".

What also works is mentorship. In fact, it's one of the best ways to train behaviour. Over a three-month period, a new hire will learn about her benefits package, figure out who's who, begin to understand the nature of her role within the organization, start to make other inroads, and so on. But if she's set up with mentors, other successful people, your new hire will mimic and mirror their behaviours. I recently came across a great mentorship program after meeting with Toronto-based Kinross, a growth leader among gold producers, employing 7,500 people worldwide and having mines and development projects in Canada, the United States, Brazil, Chile, Ecuador, Russia, Mauritania, and Ghana.

As an organization, Kinross believes that leadership training is critical to its success; in 2009, for example, the company provided 5,184 hours of leadership training to more than 200 managers and supervisors. It also has a program called "Generation Gold", which offers high-performing university graduates a four-year employment commitment featuring international work assignments, mentoring, and other professional development opportunities.[3] Clearly this is an organization that values mentorship.

"Making Partner: A Mentor's Guide to the Psychological Journey," an article published in 2000 by then Harvard professor Herminia Ibarra, also emphasizes the importance of mentorship. Ibarra studied 35 individuals who were aspiring to make partner at various professional services firms. Those who successfully made the leap did so by observing role models (such as the partners of their firm) and by emulating their behaviours—albeit, in the case of those that were successful, by emulating a combination of behaviours that suited their own personal styles (what Ibarra refers to as a "collage approach").[4]

Ibarra notes that when mentoring, senior leaders need to understand that their role is to guide young professionals—using a combination of communication and emotional and practical support—all the while recognizing that their mentees are observing their behaviours and experimenting with what works best for them. This is a key role for senior leaders to play.

The point of Ibarra's study is that mentees in the firm became even more successful by imitating—mimicking and mirroring—certain behaviours that they observed in the partners. I have spent my life as a mentee, and I know that this is true. Now, as a mentor and as a parent, I see how important the other side is and how much impact it has on people.

In your own organization, if you mentor, coach, and develop your new talent in this way, if you expose these individuals to as many different styles as possible (because really, these should be different styles of the same kinds of behaviour), and if you have them work with as many high performers in the organization as possible, guess what? You are now training for fit.

Training for Fit

Training and development budgets are usually the first to take a hit when times are tough. If they do spend the money, organizations tend to dedicate their resources to skills training, even though not much happens. Development training—which is about developing an individual, as opposed to developing the individual's skill set—is especially vulnerable to the chopping block, because the ROI is not immediate. But it is by far the more strategic of the two.

Keep this in mind: training for fit—a true development program—doesn't require expensive outsourced consultants with big titles. Why?

First, because, as outlined previously, it's not that hard. Second, by the very nature of what I've described, the whole process of training for fit takes place in-house. Your new hires learn the behaviours of your existing top performers by observing them in action. Why would you even consider outsourcing this type of training?

Training for fit starts by exposing your new hires to the highest performers that you can. It continues with the repeated articulation of the key pillars of your organization's culture. It's reinforced over the short and long term by other things, like catching your new hires doing things right—and rewarding and recognizing them for that behaviour.

A great example of a training program that reinforces behaviour is Maple Leaf Foods' Leadership Academy. The program was developed with the Richard Ivey School of Business at the University of Western Ontario.

Wayne Johnson, retired senior vice president and chief human resources officer of Maple Leaf Foods, says that the original objective of the program was to make people better—and not just by increasing their competencies, but also by instilling the organization's values.

The program has been in operation for approximately 12 years, and the company puts about 40 people through it annually—often new hires, but there's also a focus on sending top performers. The programs range from the functionally focused to, as Johnson told me, "The history of Maple Leaf, the 'why' of the values and what you need to know to thrive at Maple Leaf". About 60 percent of the time, someone from Maple Leaf is leading the course, with an Ivey faculty member taking the other 40 percent.[5]

Adds Johnson regarding Michael McCain's role: "No Ivey program gets run without Michael attending at least one day and delivering one module".

Culture can mature and grow through other ongoing development programs and events that reinforce behaviour: think of Hunter Harrison's Hunter Camps, where dozens of front-line supervisors and other leaders within the organization listened and interacted with the CEO, and talked about how culture change would be achieved at CN. Or, think of WestJet's Culture Connections, where the executive team and groups of WestJetters get together to talk about their culture. WestJet sees these sessions as an opportunity to "re-energize the emotional commitment that is so important to our culture of success". Pretty heady stuff! But I've been fortunate enough to have been invited to one of these sessions, and they're quite remarkable — not to mention a lot of fun. (There's not one person in the room who's not wearing a button that says "Care": they care, because owners care.) Both Culture Connections and Hunter Camps are great examples of how training for fit and reinforcing behaviours is an ongoing process; in fact, it should be a never-ending objective.

The point is, you start with great raw material and you make it better by focusing on the ways we know people learn — by observing the behaviour of others. Training for fit starts the minute a new hire walks in the door. From then on, everything you do, in terms of this critical form of ongoing development, should be linked to who you are as an organization.

Saying that training for fit is not possible is garbage; it works. Why shouldn't it be used more commonly in business?

Chapter 7

Culture and Celebration:
How Celebration and Rituals
Impact Culture

Celebrate what you want to see more of.

—THOMAS J. PETERS

BACK IN THE 1990S, I was an executive vice president at Halifax, Nova Scotia–based CCL Group. CCL is a consortium of independently managed companies, focusing on marketing and communications—public affairs and advertising, and also contact centres, video production, and event staging. It has more than 600 employees, and it's also an organization founded by my brother Steve, who is currently chairman and CEO.[1]

The culture at CCL was great, and Steve played a big role in ensuring that this was the case. One of his brainchilds was a regular monthly event we held called "98s".

The number 98 referred to a nonbillable code in our ad and PR division (for internal projects and new business, that kind of thing). So calling the event a "98" was a play on words, and the party itself was for the folks on the PR and professional services side of the business. Had we been in Quebec, a little after-work shindig like this would have been called a "5-à-7": a short happy hour–type event (although the parties rarely ended by 7 p.m.).

The 98s had different themes and sometimes included giveaways and/or some form of employee recognition award. Often, there was recognition of a well-done campaign, and one of the higher-ups (usually a manager or a team leader, or sometimes Steve) would talk about what had been done and who at the firm had been involved in it—like a show-and-tell. Those who were more hands-on would then come to the front of the room and talk about a particular PR or crisis communications campaign: what happened, how it was dealt with, what were the challenges and the outcomes—that kind of thing. Suppliers and clients were also invited to our 98s; these events weren't always just for employees. Maybe there was a giveaway—a coupon or gift certificate from the client, perhaps.

The point is, at a 98, there was always a show of work and a discussion of it, there were always drinks, there was always food, and there was often a specific theme (sometimes something that was more fun, and sometimes something that was relevant to what was being reinforced). People always had a good time at these events; they were always special, and they always brought people together. The 98s worked for CCL also because of the business it was in and because of the demographics of its employees.

In short, 98s had the all the makings of an organizational celebration that reinforced and aligned culture at CCL. Steve was way ahead of his time with respect to his thinking on culture. He taught me a lot about the impact of events of this type. The people at CCL wanted to get together to celebrate great work. They knew that these achievements were valued, and they were proud of their accomplishments. Clients and suppliers witnessed—live—how this work was valued. I believe that they, in turn, wanted to be associated with a firm that was committed to great work.

Celebrate What's Important

In our personal and family lives, we celebrate things that are important to us (birthdays, anniversaries, or other milestones, or religious holidays), and those celebrations reinforce what we value. It just takes observation to find out what's important to people: look not only at what they celebrate, but at how—and why—they celebrate it.

The same principle applies to organizations.

How many company events have you held or attended? How many Christmas parties? How many golf tournaments or gala dinners? And of those, how many would you honestly say were a genuine reflection of the organization—or of your own organization—and its culture?

If we believe that celebration is a form of cultural alignment (which we do), partying for partying's sake just doesn't work. Sure, a good party brings people together and creates a shared experience, and that's a good start. But if an event of that nature does nothing to reinforce the core elements of the culture—for example, how you want people to behave— then it misses the mark. To reinforce and align your culture, your organization's celebrations—which are a key alignment tool—have to be relevant to who you are as an organization.

Here are four key considerations in that process.

1. Make Celebrations about Reinforcing Core Values

A celebration is a ritual. Some of us might celebrate on our own, but celebrations are typically rituals practiced by a group. Moreover, celebrations demonstrate and reinforce core values. The organizations that truly understand this when they're planning and preparing for their own celebrations and events will do a better job at aligning their culture with those events in the process.

For instance, look at WestJet's profit-sharing celebrations: they are held at different bases all over the country, and the main celebration at the airline's hangar in Calgary attracts close to 3,000 employees. The format is very clear—in fact, the prerequisite for receiving the money is that the employee is to be thanked by her immediate manager. Employees also receive a physical cheque, as opposed to a line-item deposit on their bank statements.

"It would save us a fortune if we put it in their bank account, but that would defeat the whole purpose", says WestJet's Clive Beddoe. "The handing over of the cheque, the party, the celebration—it's the opportunity to say, 'Your hard work produced for us; thank you'. It's appreciation".

In other words, this particular celebration—which is held twice a year on a regular basis—links directly back to so many aspects of WestJet's culture.

The annual WestJet Christmas party is another example of a celebration that's aligned with the airline's culture. It's on a big scale—an event of massive proportions, bringing together everyone from in-flight personnel to executives to suppliers to people that WestJet interfaces with on a regular basis (even people like me; I've been to three of these parties). With thousands of people in attendance, this event is about WestJetters having fun, poking fun at themselves, telling great stories, and recognizing people—by putting them up on the big screen or otherwise—for great service stories over the past year. What this Christmas party tells me is that WestJet is all about cooperation, having fun, and inclusiveness (and after the dinner is over, WestJetters have to pick up their own tab for the bar—a true alignment with the values of a low-cost airline!).

Celebration doesn't always have to be through parties. More organizations are using events to celebrate. Regardless, still ask yourself this question: what's your culture?

If your culture is about sports and families, like that at Boston Pizza, your events and your celebrations should reinforce that culture. The culture at Boston Pizza is also very much about support of the franchisees. To celebrate and recognize this group, Boston Pizza holds a franchisee conference every other year. And the company holds it in a place that appeals to the demographics of its franchisee group. These are people who run sports bars and family restaurants; they want to go to places in Florida, or to Palm Desert or Palm Springs, places where they can hold a conference, yes, but also where they can play a lot of golf.

Another great example is the support that Four Seasons Hotels and Resorts gives to the annual Terry Fox Run, in support of cancer research. Isadore Sharp of Four Seasons made a personal commitment to this event back in 1980, after the tragic loss of his son Christopher to cancer in 1978.[2] Over the years, the Four Seasons has been a big supporter of this event, hosting the largest Terry Fox Run site in Ontario at Toronto's

Wilket Creek Park. It's become something that now, some 20 years later, is very important to the organization and to its people because it's rooted in the Four Seasons' history.

2. Make Your Celebrations about Great Successes

Celebrations at your organization should reinforce successes; they should acknowledge your heroes and the behaviours that drove those heroes to accomplish what they did. Ideally, this means that your celebrations should recognize your top performers not just for what they accomplished, but for how they accomplished it — for how they represented the core behaviours and values of your culture.

Often these types of celebrations take the form of President's Clubs and groups of that nature. Rather than merely recognizing great performance, organizations that do this well also understand the behaviour that drove that performance.

For example, at our firm we celebrate our people through something that we call the QSVC (Quality, Service, Value, and Culture) awards. When an award is issued, either the nominator or the manager makes a point, when presenting the award, of ensuring that people understand the behaviour that drove the success. If you can reward individuals in front of their loved ones, as we sometimes do with our QSVC awards, it has that much more impact.

3. Reinforce Connections When You Celebrate

It's also important that your celebrations are designed in such a way that they strengthen the connection that individuals in your organization have with one another and with the group. It's about demonstrating what makes the group special, thereby reinforcing group dynamics and shared experiences. That, in turn, reinforces the connection, much the way shared experiences do for a family. Shared experiences have an enormous impact on culture, especially when what makes this group special is pointed out and reinforced.

I think HOOPP — the Healthcare of Ontario Pension Plan — does a great job at celebration and at creating shared experiences. This is especially critical at this organization, because its various departments—plan operations and the investment side, for instance—operate quite independently from one another and tend to work in unique functional areas (even though they're in the same office). To help bring people together, annually, HOOPP holds something called a diversity lunch, where employees will bring in dishes that reflect their cultural background. People at HOOPP value the event—it brings them together, and it is representative of the workforce. It achieves the objective of collaboration and working together.

4. Make Celebrations Symbolic

Going back to our 98s at CCL for a moment, it was not uncommon for there to be some kind of prize or giveaway at those events. Often one of the divisional leaders, or Steve Parker, the CEO, would base these on a trivia contest, and the questions were always about the clients. For instance, to win the prize, you'd have to answer a question about a particular campaign, in relation to the client—as in, can you tell me who said this, or what was done with this particular project? It was symbolic in the sense that the prizes reinforced a message that was, and is, important at CCL—clients come first. Celebrations can also be symbolic in the sense that they highlight the name of the organization, a particular division, a particular brand or logo, a credo or a mantra, or a particular theme that was chosen for an annual event.

Align Celebrations with Culture

At the beginning of the book, we talked about our annual Canada's 10 Most Admired Corporate Cultures gala and how we celebrate the annual winners. What I didn't emphasize was how we put that event together every year. In fact, we try to give the event meaning and engage our attendees by putting the onus on them to show us their culture at the event. This has resulted in a really fun night every year (it's also been described as "the Oscars of Canadian business"). Whether it's live song and dance, giveaways, or standing on chairs and cheering, what we hope the night accomplishes is not just celebration but a reinforcement of what makes a winning culture at these organizations. What we're most proud of is that each of our Canada's 10 fills its tables not just with its senior team members, but with its high performers (as well as its key clients, partners, and suppliers). What we hope that says is that they're celebrating by recognizing their best and by acknowledging what is truly important to them.

You can celebrate for celebration's sake, but the organizations that really handle celebrations well align those celebrations with their culture, with what's important to them, and with the behaviours that they are trying to recognize and reinforce. I'd also argue that when they are aligned in this way, celebrations motivate employees, thus leading to greater productivity and greater success. When celebrations are aligned with your culture, they can not only enhance the loyalty of your people but also make those same individuals work more effectively. If they're just parties for the sake of partying, celebrations can be effective in some ways—in terms of bringing people together, for instance—but they won't accomplish the objective of aligning your culture in any true sense.

It's a powerful experience to share good times with one another. If it can be organized, either formally or informally, in a way that allows you to celebrate great things, and things that are important to your culture, that's even better.

Chapter 8

What's Your Reason for Being? How Credos and Belief Statements Reinforce Culture

---

Always aim at complete harmony of thought and word
and deed. Always aim at purifying your thoughts
and everything will be well.

—Mohandas K. Gandhi

Organizations that have figured out how to make a link between their past and their present and those that have been able to understand and communicate their fundamental reason for being have a strong tool at their disposal. In fact, as we touched on briefly in Chapter 3, "The Few and the Mighty," either approach is a great tactic for aligning culture.

Credos and Mantras

Often these tools take the form of credos or mantras. A credo is a statement of belief; historically, these were used in religion (for example, the Apostles' Creed), but these days credos are often used in organizational manifestos. A mantra, loosely, is a group of words that is capable of creating a transformation. In my view, and for our purposes here, credos and mantras are really the same type of thing—and to make things easier, I'll use the term *credo*. The important thing to emphasize is that these are short, written expressions that outline the convictions, goals, responsibilities, and philosophies of an organization. Credos can instil pride and purpose within an organization, and can align or generate comprehension and interest from all audiences—both internal and external. The best credos are partly philosophical, link to organizational history, and can facilitate transformative change—provided they're relevant and meaningful.

Probably the most famous credo out there, as we touched on earlier, is the Johnson & Johnson (J&J) credo. J&J's former chairman Robert Wood Johnson, a member of the organization's founding family, crafted it himself in 1943, before J&J became a public company and long before anyone had really heard of the term *corporate social responsibility*. If you have any sort of business background, or any kind of interest in business at all, you've probably heard of or even read the J&J credo. The 300-and-some-word document is in many ways both a moral compass for the organization and a recipe for business success. The fact that it is still in use today—throughout the organization's 250 companies in 57 countries around the world[1]—is a testament to how incredibly successful it's been.

Here are a few lines from the credo, to give you a sense of its impact and timelessness:

> *We believe our first responsibility is to the doctors, nurses and patients, to mothers and fathers and all others who use our products and services. In meeting their needs everything we do must be of high quality.We must constantly strive to reduce our costs in order to maintain reasonable prices. Customers' orders must be serviced promptly and accurately. Our suppliers and distributors must have an opportunity to make a fair profit.*
>
> *We are responsible to our employees, the men and women who work with us throughout the world. . . . Compensation must be fair and adequate, and working conditions clean, orderly and safe. We must be mindful of ways to help our employees fulfill their family responsibilities. . . .*
>
> *We are responsible to the communities in which we live and work and to the world community as well. . . .*

Our final responsibility is to our stockholders. Business must make a sound profit.[2]

Again, what's unbelievable is that this credo was written in 1943 and still has so much relevance. It deals with all of J&J's stakeholders—from employees, to medical professionals, to suppliers, to the communities in which they live, and finally to its shareholders. Many will remember the Tylenol crisis in 1982, when seven people in the Chicago area died after taking cyanide-laced capsules of Extra Strength Tylenol. The manner in which J&J handled this situation has been widely regarded as a landmark case study in effective crisis communication—in fact, it's considered to be one of the best in the history of public relations. The organization placed customers first and immediately recalled the Tylenol product from store shelves—all 31 million bottles. James Burke, J&J's company chairman at the time, put himself forward as the face of the crisis, and was lauded for his forthrightness in dealing with the media[3] (in many ways, this has similarities to Michael McCain's handling of the listeria crisis that hit Maple Leaf Foods in 1998). For J&J, the credo was what it turned to, to help guide it through such a horrific situation and to help guide its behaviour during such a turbulent time.

Another great example of a credo is Four Seasons Hotels and Resorts' Golden Rule, which states simply, "to treat others as you would wish to be treated". We've talked about this at length earlier in the book, but it's worth mentioning again here because of the value this expression provides to the organization. The Golden Rule was originally instituted by founder and chairman Isadore Sharp as a driver of cultural change in the 1980s, but it stuck and was formalized throughout the organization. It became clear that it was a credo that would continue to both drive and reinforce culture as the organization expanded and grew—from a builder, to an operator and a manager of hotels all over the world—over the next 25 years. The Golden Rule works as a credo because the idea of treating others as you would wish to be treated is simple for everybody—for employees globally—to understand and to implement in their daily activities. It works, despite the fact that when Sharp originally introduced the concept, people within his own organization dismissed it as "kooky".[4]

Another example is "Our Brew", the credo of Molson Coors.

"'Our Brew' came out of the work that was done after the merger of Molson and Coors", Dave Perkins, the president and CEO of Molson Coors Canada, told me, referring to the 2005 merger. "What we were looking for postmerger was: what do we want to have in common going forward so that we can be a multinational business that still allows us to compete locally?"

The organization and its employees undertook a fairly major year-long project to answer this question—and, as Perkins says, to attempt to clarify strategy and culture, and to "mime" the DNA of each of the businesses to see what they had in common.

The result was "Our Brew".

"Our Brew set out our ambition of what size global player we wanted to be", says Perkins. "It set out what I'd call our purpose, which was really around challenging the expected to build extraordinary brands that delight the world's beer drinkers, and gave clarity to the kind of behaviours or culture that we wanted in this business that we felt would drive our results. Then we set out four major BHAGs [Big Hairy Audacious Goals] or objectives for the year 2012 that would drive performance and drive a commonality across the business".

Other credos worth noting include the one drawn from the Princess Margaret Hospital Foundation and from its leader, president and CEO Paul Alofs. As we saw in Chapter 4, Alofs applied the principles of the social enterprise to the foundation because he believed that those principles could be instrumental in building a transformational culture within not-for-profits.

To recap, social enterprise is essentially a hybrid of the best practices from both the private sector and the not-for-profit sector. One of its major principles is the idea of the creed.

According to Alofs, a creed is an organization's most valuable asset; it is what the organization's culture is built on. Like a credo, it is a set of beliefs shared by the people in an organization, and it uses bold, focused, emotive, and authentic language.

In fact under Alofs's leadership, the Princess Margaret Hospital Foundation developed a creed that is about as bold as you can get: "We are conquering cancer at Canada's cancer research hospital, The Princess Margaret. In our Lifetime."

"There was a time not long ago when cancer was a death sentence, and the treatment was dreaded almost as much as the disease", Alofs told me. "We've seen that change in our lifetime at the Princess Margaret. Yes, we are still losing people to cancer. But at the Princess Margaret we've seen a provincial cancer hospital become one of the world's top five cancer research centres. We've seen our people grow beyond 1,000. We've seen leading researchers from all over the world leave their homes to come here, because this is where they believe the fight will be finished in our lifetime. We are closing in."

"The creed is the foundation of great culture", added Alofs. "You don't have to work at a cancer foundation and you don't need to work at a not-for-profit to have deeply held and/or shared beliefs throughout your organization". Rallying people behind this creed seems to have had a major impact—in addition to the other changes that Alofs implemented at the foundation.

If credos are about who you really are and what you're all about as an organization, they can be enormously effective at helping your people connect and relate to the organization. Credos can also be transformative—like chanting a mantra. But change doesn't happen unless people have a reason to change. Paul Alofs created that reason at the foundation. Using the principles of social enterprise, he essentially created a platform that enabled his people to have a substantial impact, more than doubling the size of the annual donations that the foundation received. The transformative change at the foundation was facilitated in many ways by the creed, which people rallied behind. Why? Because it was relevant, meaningful, and powerful.

Developing Your Credo

How do you develop your own credo? Where do you start?

The first step, as we've discussed, is for organizations to have a solid understanding of the core behaviours that drive success in their organization and to understand their culture and who they are (as we've discussed, the Know Thyself principle).

From there, here are some general steps to follow:

- Assemble a small group of individuals, people who tend to take pride in the organization, and hold a brainstorming session in which you talk about who you think you are and what's really important to you as an organization. You could also go further in this process and develop larger focus groups of employees across your organization, and perhaps consider doing the same with your customers.
- This initial session could result in a draft mission and/or vision statement that includes the organization's basic philosophies, values, and even achievements.
- Once this initial document has been drawn up, regroup; throw back the original ideas and discuss them.
- Select the best and most compelling ideas, and develop a mock-up of your credo.
- Have customers, suppliers, and other key stakeholders look at it, discuss it again, and get more feedback.
- Create a final version.

The mood and the mindset of the individuals involved in this process are critical. If you want a credo to be utilized and respected, it has to evolve from a point of pride as well as from a clearly felt mandate on how you do things as an organization.

Credos have been largely usurped or taken over by vision and mission statements. A vision is where you want to be; it's a long-term stated goal. A mission is effectively how you want to act on an everyday basis in order to get there. Neither is a credo.

The purpose of a credo is to create a simple reminder of the organization's convictions, goals, and responsibilities and/or philosophy; it's meant to be a reference guide to keep an organization on course and on message. It's also something that people can rally behind, if necessary. But if a credo isn't obvious or fairly easy to come up with, it perhaps shouldn't be developed. A credo has to represent how your organization wants to act, and it has to consider all of your various audiences and stakeholders at the same time. Because we all like to be linked to our past to some degree, if a credo can connect to your organization's history, that's even better. Taking all of this into consideration creates a credo that has amazing potential as a cultural alignment tool.

Chapter 9

Measure Once and
Cut Three Times

The only man who behaved sensibly was my tailor;

he took my measurement anew every time he saw me,

while all the rest went on with their old measurements

and expected them to fit me.

—George Bernard Shaw

"Measure three times before you cut once". I call this the carpenter's mantra. It's a proverb about detail and precision, about not wasting materials or wasting time, and about not having to redo your work later.

We think the opposite is true when you're measuring culture. Yes, culture needs to be measured regularly and fairly often. And when you cut it for the first time, that "cut", if you will, needs to be made to "fit" with what is going on within your organization at that time and place. But if we argue that measuring culture is about measuring behaviour, which we believe it is, we know that behaviour is not static. It's not like measuring a 2 × 4 so that it fits into the frame of a house.

Measuring culture involves measuring it at a point in time, and it needs to be compared to reference points that indicate what the culture is in that organization at that point in the organization's life cycle. It needs to be compared with other behaviours within the organization—those in one particular division compared with those in another, or those in one functional area compared with those in another. And these reference points need to be considered vis-à-vis the broader organization. From there, the gaps need to be identified and be dealt with and/or closed. So all of that being the case, you may measure culture often, but you may also "cut" it more than once. In other words, culture should be measured constantly and "cut" or shaped for the organization for that particular point in time: from there, make your alignment tools, your systems and initiatives, support the culture and the assets of the culture.

Tools for Measuring Corporate Culture

When asked whether they measure their organization's corporate culture, 88 percent of the respondents to our 2011 Canadian Corporate Culture Study said yes. As you can see from Figure 9-1, this has changed drastically since 2006, when only 35 percent of respondents indicated that they measured corporate culture.

It's interesting to note what our respondents say when we ask them *how* they measure culture. Figure 9-2 gives the results from 2011.

In fact, 78 percent of the respondents chose employee engagement (or employee attitude) surveys as their preferred method of measuring culture within their organization. As you'll note in the graph, cultural assessments were the preferred measurement tool of only 20 percent of the respondents to our study.

Here's my issue with the results: employee attitude surveys are great at surveying employees to get a sense of their views and issues, but they don't measure employee behaviour, and therefore they don't do a great job of measuring culture.

	Response Percent
2006	35%
2007	43%
2008	55%
2009	69%
2010	78%
2011	88%

Source: Waterstone Human Capital, "2011 Canadian Corporate Culture Study".

Figure 9-1 Percentage of Respondents Measuring Corporate Culture, 2006–2011

		Response Percent
Employee engagement surveys		78.2%
360-degree feedback		42.7%
Performance reviews		67.3%
Cultural assessments		20%
External benchmarking		28.2%
"Gut feel"		25.5%
Informal feedback from employees		65.5%

Source: Waterstone Human Capital, "2011 Canadian Corporate Culture Study".

Figure 9-2 How Do You Measure Corporate Culture?

I'll make my case by drawing an analogy or two. For example, let's look at voter turnout in the last Canadian general election (on May 2, 2011). According to Elections Canada, it was 61.4 percent. Most Canadians feel that this is far too low a turnout. But our behaviour may not reflect that attitude. For instance, if you felt that a 61.4 percent turnout was too low, would you go out and speak to your neighbour, who was too busy to vote, and encourage him to do so next time? Did you yourself even vote, or did other priorities take over on that day? The point I'm trying to make here is that attitudes don't necessarily influence behaviour. In fact, attitudes and behaviour are often far apart. Maybe your attitude towards potato chips is that they're fattening and bad for your health. But on a Friday night after a long week, when you're sitting in front of the TV relaxing, don't they taste great chased down with a cold beer?

Don't get me wrong; employee attitude surveys are valuable. They can provide snapshots of how employees feel about the culture and what their views of the organization are. But they're not measurements of behaviour. And since that's the case, they're not measuring culture. The better measurement, by far, is the cultural assessment.

Cultural Assessments

We touched on the cultural assessment briefly in Chapter 1. Our message there was about the importance of the Know Thyself principle. We discussed how a cultural assessment can help organizations take that first step on the corporate culture front by defining who they are.

But assessments are also critical tools that allow organizations to take culture to the next level. How? By providing concrete ways to measure behaviour.

Cultural assessments are essentially conversations with people. It could be with your high performers, or with a broader section of your team. In an assessment, it's important that you truly zero in on the measurement of culture by observing the behaviour of your high performers. As we discussed earlier in the book, your top performers, and the behaviours that they exhibit, can provide you with key insights.

In fact, a cultural assessment is the most effective way to identify the critical behaviours that are shared in a company. No matter how you plan to use it, it will provide key insights into the way your company works, both as a whole and by functional area.

Performing a Cultural Assessment

Step 1

The first step is an in-depth meeting with the chief executive officer and the human resource leader to discuss the existing corporate strategy,

---

The Four-Step Cultural Assessment

- **Step 1:** Discuss existing behaviours and practices with the CEO and the HR leader.
- **Step 2:** Review business plans and corporate strategy documents.
- **Step 3:** Observe behaviour—meet with the members of the executive team and with top performers across functions, divisions, locations, and organizational events to ascertain their business practices and current behavioural themes.
- **Step 4:** Perform gap analysis and present recommendations for moving the culture to its desired state.

behaviours, and values; to identify key objectives by function; and to obtain an overview of the executive team.

The key to the cultural assessment is to talk about, ask about, and ideally spend time watching people's behaviour. Before beginning that process, an in-depth review of the current situation with the CEO and with the organization's HR leader is in order. What kinds of behavioural themes exist among top performers? Which behaviours are rewarded? Which are reprimanded? Is behaviour measured formally, as it is in the organizations we've previously discussed, such as Yellow Media Inc. and Maple Leaf Foods, or is it an informal measure?

Step 2

The next step is a review of business plans, corporate strategy documents, and/or departmental annual plans.

Before you begin the process of observing behaviour, you first need to develop a thorough understanding of the organization's financial situation, business objectives, and performance goals. This is critical, because you need to understand whether the objectives and the vision are clearly stated and whether either of them is in conflict with the behaviours that are taking place. What is already being communicated about the vision of the organization? Is it actually being used? At this stage of the assessment, asking the organization's leaders these types of questions is very important.

Step 3

The third step is to hold meetings with each identified member of the executive and senior leadership team (vice presidents and directors) and with top performers and others across functions, divisions, locations, and lines of business. The aim of these meetings is to ascertain business practices and current behavioural themes (real and desired, as well as those that are currently practiced).

The best way to conduct these observations is by gaining access to the organization's day-in and day-out activities, by going to functions, by participating in meetings, and by noting customs—essentially, by observing how the organization does things. Or perhaps it's by attending a special event. In one instance where we were hired to conduct a cultural assessment, the client happened to invite me to a multicultural dinner that it was hosting. It was a perfect opportunity to observe behaviour, gave us more information for the assessment, and ultimately informed our work.

In the process of conducting a cultural assessment, don't stop at the head office or at the CEO's chair. Be sure to look at and observe behaviours at various locations, within various divisions, and within different functional areas. What's valued? What's rewarded? What isn't? If possible, discussing these questions with the organization's board chair or other members is also useful.

Step 4

The final step is to perform a gap analysis, both for the organization as a whole and for each major function, location, division, and line of business. These findings are then presented with recommendations for moving the organization's culture to its desired state.

A cultural assessment should ultimately provide a gap analysis. This analysis should first outline both the stated culture of the organization and the culture that the organization desires. Next in the analysis comes the reality check—an outline of the culture that the organization actually has (division by division, function by function, regional office by regional office), noting if and where any subcultures exist. Finally, there should be a look at the discrepancies between the two: what kind of culture the organization wants versus what kind of culture the organization has. The key here is to mark where the gaps exist, because that's where potential solutions lie. Organizations then need to develop tactics either to close those gaps or to understand what they can do to make things different.

Almost always, gaps have been created by the leaders of a particular division or function, or, in fact, even by the leader of the company. (As we've noted, if you really want to understand the culture of an organization, take a good look at how the leader behaves.) If you're noticing a certain type of common behaviour among a particular group of people in a particular division of a company, for instance, the chances are good that they're picking up that behaviour from the leader of that division.

In one of our more recent cultural assessment assignments, we noticed a very consistent behaviour among the executives of the company—with the exception of one department. Unlike the behaviour in the rest of the organization, the behaviour within this one department was divisive, and two camps had sprung up. A new leader was at the helm and had essentially created these two camps by bringing in new people and allowing those newbies to be judged by a different set of behaviours, thus alienating the others. The point here is that the divisive behaviour was created by the leader. Despite attempts by the CEO's office and by HR to correct the situation, nothing changed. A new leader is now in place, and I can almost assure you that the problem within that department doesn't exist anymore. Why? Because the new leader acts within the boundaries of the expressed and desired culture of the organization.

Cultural Assessments Provide Real Information

Cultural assessments can lead to concrete solutions. Since it is based on an analysis of behaviour, what you're getting from a cultural assessment is real information about your culture—complete with strategies for improvement. The cultural assessment goes far beyond the employee engagement survey, which might provide you only with responses along the lines of employees saying things like: "I think our culture is great!" Again, it's good to have this kind of information, but it's not going to give you actual measurements of behaviour, nor will the results of an employee engagement survey arm you with a plan to make things better. The real value of engagement surveys is seeing what employees think of the organization and of its management at a particular point in time. However, it's not a true measurement of culture.

How and Why Cultural Assessments Work

The reality is that cultural assessments work because people find it easier to talk about how others act than about how they themselves are acting. If you're asking the top performers within a particular division to tell you about the behaviours of others, in general, they'll tell you. From there, themes will develop. As the third party conducting the assessment, your job then becomes to analyze those themes.

Third parties—firms like ours or other consulting organizations—should always be the ones to perform a cultural assessment because they have no inherent bias. The HR department can't take on the task—not because it's necessarily biased, but because that department also needs to be assessed.

How often should cultural assessments take place? For some organizations, it's enough to perform this exercise annually, because of the time commitment involved (usually about four to six weeks, depending on the availability of the executive team); others, depending on their internal issues, should consider a biannual cultural assessment. Anything more frequent than that would probably be overkill.

If you've ever read anything on corporate culture, you'll know that the seminal book on the topic is the 1992 work *Corporate Culture and Performance* by John Kotter and James Heskett. Kotter and Heskett talk about the differences between adaptive and unadaptive cultures. In the former, "managers throughout the hierarchy should provide leadership to initiate change in strategies and tactics whenever necessary to satisfy the legitimate interests of not just stockholders, or customers, or employees, but all three". In unadaptive cultures, "the norm is that managers behave cautiously to protect or advance themselves, their product, or their immediate work groups."[1]

Kotter and Heskett are effectively saying that in adaptive cultures, organizations have figured out that they need to facilitate the adoption of practices and strategies that respond to changing markets and to new environments—and to changes in culture. In fact, organizations that can change and adapt create healthy cultures. In the case of a cultural assessment, for instance, those organizations would take that information and say: "Okay, we need to make these changes in this area". Conversely, unhealthy or unadaptive cultures are more arrogant; they're inward-focused, and they're not interested in changing. In the case of a cultural assessment, for instance, these organizations would be loath to admit that any differences, or any subcultures, exist internally, preferring to stick with the party line that the entire organization is on the same page. Second, unadaptive cultures will rarely want to change. These organizations won't alter who they are in order to change the cultural context, nor will they purge their organization of leaders or high performers who, through their behaviour, are creating a poisonous environment.

Conclusion

To truly measure culture, you need to observe behaviour on a regular—at minimum, annual—basis. Spend time with your high performers to truly understand what's valued and what the common themes within that sector are, and to find out how these people behave in order to get things done successfully in your organization. Whether this takes place via a cultural assessment, through executive interviews or focus groups, or simply by talking about it and observing how people behave within your organization, you'll be armed with more concrete information about the state of your organization's culture.

Chapter 10

Culture Killers: Tips and Tricks for Identifying Things That Can Hurt Corporate Culture

---

I couldn't repair your brakes,
so I made your horn louder.

—Steven Wright

THERE ARE A NUMBER of things that can have a really negative effect on culture, some of them quickly and others over time.

Ten Most Common Corporate Culture Killers

- Lack of consistency or split personality leadership
- Misalignment of systems or processes within the business
- Mishandled mergers and acquisitions
- New leadership—too much, too fast
- Doubt and negativity
- Neglecting culture in expansion mode
- Noncore business distractions
- Accepting bad behaviour from high performers
- Letting your culture go stale—not evolving
- Sacrificing culture during tough times

---

1. Lack of Consistency or Split Personality Leadership

When we asked respondents to our annual Canadian Corporate Culture Study to give us their personal definition of corporate culture, in 2011, 85 percent said that corporate culture is defined by "the values and behaviours of leaders".[1] Similarly, 92 percent said that their current leadership has led to the evolution of their corporate culture.[2]

Obviously, and as we've talked about in this book, leadership has an enormous influence on corporate culture, for better, as discussed in Chapter 4, or for worse. In the latter case, leaders can kill culture in many ways: it may be marred by bad behaviour, made confusing by a series of different leaders over time, or simply be unpredictable and inconsistent.

Essentially, given that culture is so heavily influenced by leadership, when the leadership changes, or when it changes its voice without clear alignment or without a clear operational structure (or the systems to support it), there is a loss of consistency; the message is watered down, and it becomes confusing to employees and stakeholders alike.

In successful organizations with strong cultures, there is consistency at the top. That doesn't necessarily mean that the CEO has been there for eons, but it does mean that the organization has benefited from an evolving culture or from a culture that has been very consistent over time. A great example is Tim Hortons. Despite the recent change in CEO, this is an organization with an extraordinarily stable executive team. As Brigid Pelino, the senior vice president of human resources at Tim Hortons, told me recently, the tone from the top is key to maintaining that consistent culture—even as the organization experiences extraordinary growth.

"As you grow larger, the dependence on distributed leadership becomes higher. So the need for those leaders to really embody the values of the original leaders becomes critical, or else you can't do it", says Pelino. "I think the tone comes from the top, always. I've always believed the culture reflects the personality of the CEO".

Another great example is a big institution like Johnson & Johnson (J&J), where I started my career and where the culture doesn't change. Through J&J's "Our Credo", employees get a real sense of both the organization's history and its culture. There is a sense of belonging to something bigger. The credo has been incredibly successful. 68 years after it was first written, it is still in use throughout the organization's 250 companies across 57 countries around the world. Even Microsoft can be used as an example here. The transition of authority from Bill Gates to Steve Balmer in 2000 worked as it was planned, and it represented the culture. The message from the top was consistent and was focused on who the company was at the time and what its culture meant.

There are lots of examples of leaders who go wrong. This can happen in public institutions—clearly, Eliot Spitzer couldn't stay on as governor of New York because he didn't represent the values of the office and, more important, he didn't represent how individuals who hold that office should behave. In the private sector, a great example is Parmalat. When its founder, Calisto Tanzi, started to get the company into trouble (he was prosecuted for it eventually), it became clear that Parmalat didn't know who it was or what it stood for as an organization. In each of these cases, inconsistent leadership was detrimental to the organization's culture, and to the organization as a whole.

2. Misalignment of Systems or Processes within the Business

The most common culture killer is misalignment of systems. The organization has the right tone and messages from the top, but there are issues down the line that are causing problems. Most commonly, this happens because the systems that were designed to support the organization at a different or earlier time have not been upgraded or changed to deal with the organization in its current state. A common example is an organization that claims to have a performance-based culture but doesn't have the compensation systems to support it. We run into this frequently in our practice.

A great example of an organization that figured out the importance of aligning its compensation systems in order to drive performance is Yellow Media Inc. In the next chapter, we'll talk more about Yellow Media and how the culture at that organization has changed. But the general point I'll make here is this: back in 2003, the organization inherited a culture that wasn't necessarily performance-driven, and it knew from the get-go that if it was to be successful, that had to change.

First, a bit of background.

Yellow Media Inc., which bills itself as Canada's number one Internet company and a leading performance media and marketing solutions company, employs 4,143 people and has three companies under its umbrella: Yellow Pages Group (YPG), Trader Corporation, and Canpages.[3] Back in 2002—and through the most important management leveraged buyout in Canadian history—the company acquired Bell ActiMedia and became an independent company; it completed an IPO in 2003.[4]

At the helm all this time has been Marc Tellier, president and CEO of YPG and CEO of both Trader and Canpages.

"Bell ActiMedia, the predecessor business to Yellow Pages that we inherited, had a culture of self-entitlement", Tellier told me recently. "A culture that easily accepted defeat, where people felt they were entitled to things because they had tenure or had been there a while. We inherited whatever culture Bell had, which—quite frankly—was misunderstood and miscommunicated, and people didn't live it or understand it".

Tellier also inherited a sales force that was 75 percent unionized.[5] As one of his many tactics to address culture at the new company, Tellier initiated a performance-based compensation system, and was very successful in doing so—even in that unionized environment. His success had to do with how the new values and behaviours of the organization were communicated and aligned throughout the organization (again, something we'll learn more about in the next chapter), but it also had to do with how performance was assessed.

At Yellow Media, half of an employee's performance appraisal is based on the results that he accomplished, using established metrics. The other half is based on how he did it. In other words, Yellow Media wanted to instil and align a culture in which its people were also rewarded for living the organization's stated values.

"We're about as performance-oriented as they come", said Tellier. "But the 'how' is as important as the 'what'".

This is a great example of how an organization can align its systems and processes to drive results, all the while reinforcing its culture. You've got to have systems that support the culture, not the other way around. And it's also about how you look at performance. Yellow Media's breakaway from Bell is one of those enormous success stories for an organization. Under Tellier's leadership, this is now a company that has almost 60 percent profitability. Today, that profitability is still at an all-time high. While the marketplace isn't rewarding it in terms of the share price, the performance is still there. It's an organization that spends 50 percent of its performance measurement on measuring behaviour. Even though the stock performance hasn't been rewarding, the company is still performing exceedingly well.

The Importance of Recognition

Another great way to ensure that your systems are aligned with your culture is to catch people doing things right. Recognizing your people publicly has a great impact on culture, more so than rewarding those individuals. One-on-one support and mentoring is also critical, as we saw in our discussion of Herminia Ibarra's "Making Partner" study in Chapter 6. It's also important that you give your top performers new opportunities. In fact, our Canadian Corporate Culture Study revealed that 82 percent of respondents feel that the best way to retain their top talent is by keeping people challenged (see Figure 10-1).[6] Doing so cultivates leadership, rewards their previous behaviour and performance, and allows them to have the chance to further succeed—or fail.

Some organizations do this really well. They develop their leaders and then recognize them for their success rather than punishing them all

	Response Percent
Higher compensation	31.0%
Better benefits	30.0%
Advancement opportunities	77.3%
Career development	74.5%
CSR policy aligned to employee goals	18.2%
Empowerment	60.0%
Keeping them challenged	82.0%
Work-life balance and wellness initiatives	60.0%
Noncompete agreement	1.8%
Training and development	74.5%

Source: Waterstone Human Capital, "2011 Canadian Corporate Culture Study".

Figure 10-1 How Do You Retain Top Talent?

the time for failing. The key is to align your systems so that they support and train the people within your organization in living certain behaviours, and then to recognize those behaviours. GE did enormously well at this under Jack Welch. Welch built GE's culture around Six Sigma and around the idea of being first or second in every market. And although Six Sigma is based on the operating principle of being lean and trying to be the leader, it also shaped behaviours. That's what drove the culture change and led to success, which Jeff Immelt has taken to the next level. The systems were aligned to support the culture.

3. Mishandled Mergers and Acquisitions

Mergers and acquisitions (M&As) can kill your culture. What typically kills you in an M&A is not that you find out that the assets weren't what you thought they'd be, it's that the two cultures don't fit together. In fact, far too often, when organizations are considering this type of growth, they don't bother with a cultural assessment, and as a result, they don't know what the cultural differences between themselves and the company that they have newly acquired or merged with are. We often do this kind of work, and at the very least, we will try to make organizations aware of what the gaps are and which ones can and can't be closed.

A merger or an acquisition could be the quickest way to kill your culture because at the end of the day, you're not really merging two cultures—one is taking over the other. The questions for the organization that is leading the charge are really as follows: what are you adopting from the new culture, and what are you not willing to tolerate? Having the answers to these questions is critical to the success of the organization moving forward.

When considering a merger or an acquisition, organizations should examine the synergies. Furthermore, in the communication of the deal to existing and new employees, there should also be a concerted effort to focus on similarities, like core behaviours. At the end of the day, people will rally around things that are similar to what they already have if they know what those things are.

Lastly, organizations in this position need to take a long, hard look at the cultural differences and determine what the new culture is going to be. If necessary, from here, new and updated systems should be developed to support that culture.

It's crucial to remember that M&As have the power to kill your culture, and it's not because you've acquired bad assets. It's because you haven't done a good enough job of thoughtfully assessing the acquired culture. This further underscores the need to conduct cultural assessments.

4. New Leadership—Too Much, Too Fast

When asked if a new leader can change corporate culture, 88 percent of respondents to our 2011 Canadian Corporate Culture Study said yes (see Figure 10-2).[7]

Clearly, leaders can change the culture of an organization. But it's not always for the better. In fact, new leadership can be a culture killer because when a new leader, or new leadership, comes on board, what you're doing is importing a new culture to the organization. If this is done too quickly, it can have a negative effect.

The issue, of course, is that it takes time for an organization as a whole to change. Over time, companies have done things a certain way, and now all of a sudden a new leader says, "This is how we shall behave". It's a tough transition, especially for long-standing organizations.

When a new leader comes on board, sets a new tone from the top, and is looking to either import a new culture or change the existing one, it's critical that she have a plan in place to allow for the evolution of that change—particularly the change in behaviour. The plan should also

		Response Percent
Yes	▬▬▬▬▬▬▬▬▬	87.5%
No	▬▬▬	12.5%

Source: Waterstone Human Capital, "2011 Canadian Corporate Culture Study".

Figure 10-2 Do You Believe a New Leader Can Change Your Corporate Culture?

identify who can change, how quickly they can do it, who needs to go, and what systems there need to be to support those decisions. If you do all this too quickly, it will become an enormously difficult process. Leaders can't change an entire company at once; they can't change out all of the people. It's just not feasible.

Doing an assessment to gain a full understanding of what needs to happen and when is critical. I often caution leaders to communicate that change—for example, the new vision and the new reality—only after a significant amount of time has passed. So what does "significant" mean in this case? Is it three months; is it six months? It's not 30 days, let's put it that way. Every organization is unique, and you should determine the appropriate amount of time accordingly. The key is to understand what you want to do, define where you want to go, and then articulate what the new culture is going to be when you get there. Doing all of this too quickly can be a real culture killer.

5. Doubt and Negativity

When people in an organization doubt the viability of the culture or are negative towards it, this can be a real culture killer. Often this happens during an acquisition, or when there is another significant change, like the changing of a CEO or of a major shareholder. Regardless, when the organization faces doubt and negativity, it's a problem. And it's one that the leadership needs to recognize and deal with right away.

Doubt and negativity can often emerge when new leaders come on board—either from the outside or internally. The way this is handled is crucial. If we want to look at how to do it right, look no further than Katie Taylor's transition from chief operating officer to chief executive officer of Four Seasons Hotels and Resorts. As Taylor told me recently: "I think whenever there is change, regardless of the kind it is—corporate, ownership, geographic—the task for senior leadership is to get out ahead of it and say, 'Okay, what are the possible implications for the culture; what are the things that might come through the employee filter that might make them nervous?'" She further notes that one of the most important things that happened when she became the CEO of Four Seasons was the manner in which the founder and chairman, and her predecessor, Isadore Sharp, implemented and communicated that change.

"He told people three years before that it was going to happen, and he gave them plenty of time to get used to the idea", says Taylor. "And Issy was smart enough to anoint me, if I can use that term, at a time when he was still vibrant and around. He handpicked me, and it wasn't something that was born out of a crisis. It was part of a very long-term plan and therefore was viewed as very culturally consistent".

What you saw in the case of Katie Taylor was a very structured, paced, thoughtful change, and as a result, fear, doubt, and negativity were mitigated. This is not always the case, and leadership changes can often be abrupt. When this happens, it's important to take stock of the changes that are taking place at the cultural level. Conduct assessments at the 6- and 18-month points to determine the gaps between the transformation that's actually happening and what was expected and hoped for on the cultural front.

We often get asked in our business: should we promote from the inside or go outside? And the answer really is this: if you have the talent within the organization, and if you have the ability to cultivate it and allow it to take shape, over time, promoting from within is always the better choice. Also, fear-based change will not work; it's been proven time and time again that fear is not a great motivator when it comes to cultural change. Like the turnaround coach in sports, fear will create short-term change only. It might have an impact at the time, but it will rarely stick.

6. Neglecting Culture in Expansion Mode

Too much expansion too fast, without paying attention to your culture, can be a culture killer. Organizations have done this differently, and we're going to examine this in detail in Chapter 13, but for our purposes here, let me say this: if you expand without considering your organization's culture, you will compromise what's made you successful. Business expansion for expansion's sake with no attention paid to how you're going to export some of your culture and import what works in the local market can land you in trouble on both ends.

7. Noncore Business Distractions

Noncore business distractions can affect your culture. Essentially, these involve situations in which either the CEO or the organization's leadership gets distracted. Sometimes the distractions are personal, perhaps involving failed marriages or family or personal illnesses. In other instances, CEOs can be distracted by things like vanity projects (for lack of a better term). Take RIM, for instance. Co-CEO Jim Balsillie became focused on bringing an NHL team to Canada, first with his bid for the Pittsburgh Penguins in 2006 and then with his attempt to bring the Phoenix Coyotes to Hamilton, Ontario, in 2008 and 2009.[8] In addition, with a series of alleged patent infringement lawsuits and questions surrounding stock options, RIM's leadership is continually being distracted from its core business, and it's probably no surprise that its market share and its stock are suffering as a result.

The reality is that if you have a noncore business distraction that's affecting the day-to-day behaviour of your people or that's leading you to take your eye off the ball, it will affect your culture.

8. Accepting Bad Behaviour from High Performers

What do you do when your high performers are exhibiting behaviours that are contrary to the kinds of behaviour that are accepted and recognized within your organization? Do you fire your top salesperson, or your top biller, because in the course of doing her job, she alienates and offends people and doesn't exhibit the behaviours that you as a leader have established?

Conversely, if you've created a culture of openness and communication, and one of your people comes to you to tell you in confidence about the unacceptable behaviour of another one of your top-performing people, how do you handle it? If you ignore that confidence and the information that it contains—for the sake of higher sales, for instance—what kind of message does that send?

Neither is an easy situation. But accepting bad behaviour for the sake of your bottom line is a culture killer.

Thomas Dimitroff, current general manager of the Atlanta Falcons and two-time NFL executive of the year, is in the midst of what he called atmospheric cultural change at the Atlanta Falcons under owner Arthur Blank. Tom is a former college football teammate of mine, and in my view, he's also one of the most principled and disciplined people I have ever met.

I asked Dimitroff recently about all the changes that have come to the organization. I said: "Tom, you've made all these changes. You have had to deal with the Michael Vick situation and other major personal and management decisions—what do you do if a high performer—a player, a coach, or a member of the management team—is acting contrary to your new culture at the Falcons?"

He said: "Marty, we cut him. We get rid of him, right away, no questions asked".

I said: "Simple as that?" He said: "Simple as that. Because if you don't do that, you're accepting it, and it's a new standard. It's like saying, 'Here's how we won't act, but if we do act this way, well, we'll accept it'".

Getting rid of top performers because of behaviour that runs counter to your organization's culture is not easy, but it's a defining moment. Making the hard decision to let someone go or to deal with the behaviour in a concrete way sends a strong message. Unfortunately, you may know that those are the right decisions only if they're applauded after the fact—like in situations where your culture is challenged, but it comes out the winner. You also know as a leader that when people come to you in confidence to say, "I think we've got a problem", your culture is strong—based on that individual's behaviour.

9. Letting Your Culture Go Stale—Not Evolving

Organizations may be proud of their culture, and they're right to feel that way, but if they don't pay attention to the evolution of that culture over time, it could come back to haunt them.

As the president and CEO of Four Seasons, Katie Taylor feels that it is her job to ensure that the culture of the organization—and its famous Golden Rule, to treat others as you would wish to be treated—stays vibrant and stays relevant.

"The more powerful a culture becomes, the more it can become an excuse for why you can't do a whole lot of things. Which stops evolution", Taylor told me. "Culture sometimes can become inwardly focused. If you think of the beginning of our culture, it was so we could flow this caring attitude out to a guest who would pay a lot of money for a superior product, driving superior profitability of the business. But there is this side of the culture that says, 'Treat others the way I want to be treated', and the 'I want to be treated' part can become a very inward-looking part of the culture. We're constantly adjusting the thought process around the culture to make sure it is outward looking".

10. Sacrificing Culture during Tough Times

One of the greatest challenges to organizational cultures in recent times was probably the Great Recession of 2008–2009. How do you keep your culture healthy when layoffs and economic uncertainty all of a sudden become the norm? The best organizations look to their culture—rely on it and stubbornly refuse to sacrifice it—to help them survive tough times. And in the end, they come out in a better position because of that approach.

"As soon as the going gets tough, people say no, no—it should all be about profit. You shouldn't be paying people an incentive for holding the ship together, for investing in the culture, for investing in the human capital", the Four Seasons' Katie Taylor told me. "I have to say I disagree. Those are the times when you need those values most, not least. Everybody can be great to their employees and throw lots of events and have lots of perks and benefits for the staff when the coffers are full. Try making something out of nothing culturally when the business is under financial pressure".

The recession was very tough on the hospitality industry, and the Four Seasons was not immune to the pressures. But as Taylor points out, the manner in which the situation was handled (the "how") could not have happened without the organization's strong culture.

Taylor said: "We had to do a lot of layoffs during the Great Recession, because the downturn was so sharp. Unlike 9/11, it was long and deep—we knew this was going to be a multiyear crisis. But we reminded our managers: it's not what you're doing, it's how you're doing it. So as a company, we made a master list of every manager who was laid off, and we put hiring freezes in place at every hotel regardless of its circumstances so that we could transfer people who were able to move from one place to another to keep them employed".

Taylor mentioned that the organization created a database of the individuals who were displaced during the crisis, and that this is still the first source that the Four Seasons turns to when there is an opening. At the end of 2010, the organization had rehired 20 percent of the people who had been laid off. The main goal, Taylor said, is to keep in touch, to keep these individuals as a part of the family.

The end result?

"Our overall RevPAR [revenue per available room] improved in 2010 at twice the industry average—across the globe", said Taylor. "My theory? And I say it to the staff every time I visit a hotel—the customers knew the difference, and they're voting with their wallets. We didn't change, other people did, and when the business came back and they could afford to choose an experience for their business or for their leisure, they chose us because we stayed true to our values".

WestJet's Ferio Pugliese also credits the airline's culture for helping the organization through a very difficult time.

"At the end of the day, we had an executive team that was grappling and scared about the whole recession, what was happening, knowing that if things didn't improve, we'd be in the position where we'd possibly have to face layoffs—something the company had never done", Pugliese told me. "The first order of business was, 'Let's not hide behind this; we're a culture of ownership, that's what we've built, let's use that to our advantage, let's go out and tell people what's going on'. So we did".

Pugliese says that transparency was key—the executives met with the employee association and told the employees what was happening: how much revenue was dropping, how much demand had decreased, and that if revenue or demand hit certain levels, there were certain things that would need to be considered. The message: the executive would exhaust all voluntary measures before cutting into the heart of WestJet—its people.

"Somebody said to me—'Good or bad, just tell me. I want to know. We don't like the message, we don't like what we see, we don't like the potential outcomes, but we appreciate that you're honest. Because you know what? We see it too. We're just waiting for someone to come and validate it for us'", Pugliese recalled from a conversation with an employee. "So it's all transparency. I think with good leadership that's transparent, you can overcome any challenge".

The "All Eyes on Cost" initiative emerged from that period, in order to find cost savings that would have the least impact on employees. One of the most innovative ideas came from a flight attendant: she encouraged her colleagues to reuse their personal water bottles. It was an idea that wound up saving the airline $90,000 a year. I would make the argument that it was a concept that worked because it was true to the WestJet culture of ownership and of focusing on cost and efficiencies.

Chapter 11

Culture Change: Changing Habits, Systems, and People

*Culture does not change because we desire
to change it. Culture changes when the organization
is transformed; the culture reflects the realities of
people working together every day.*

—Frances Hesselbein

When Court Carruthers first joined Acklands-Grainger in 2002 as
the vice president of national accounts and sales, it didn't take long for
him to realize that the then nearly 115-year-old company was punching
below its weight.

In fact, to Carruthers, Acklands-Grainger was a sleeping giant.

"When I got here in 2002, what was very obvious was that people
were committed to service for the customer—there was a great passion,
and it was well-embedded", Carruthers told me as I sat down for an interview in April with both him and Sean O'Brien, who was named president of Acklands-Grainger in 2009. "At the same time, there was a very
clear understanding that we were the biggest player in our industry, but
we weren't really hitting our potential".

The question became: if Acklands-Grainger was already the biggest
player in Canada in the industrial, safety, and fastener products business,
what would it take for it to become the undisputed leader?

To Carruthers, a stronger corporate culture was a big part of that answer. And when he became president of the organization in 2006, he thought the timing was right to make his move. But this wasn't about radical, extensive change. This was about implementing key strategic initiatives designed specifically to wake the giant.

"If you try to take something that is at one end of the spectrum and move it all the way to the other end of the spectrum, I'm not sure you can do that. That's a multidecade proposition", he said. "There wasn't this idea of having to completely shift this old culture that didn't want to be shifted; this was really a situation of making a corporation more open and more flexible and really tapping into the latent culture that was already there".

He added: "There was this passion to serve customers, but at the same time this frustration that the company wasn't making it easy to do that. So processes that didn't work well, that were maybe overly cumbersome or overly bureaucratic—our size was making us slow and not responsive in the local marketplace.

"Everyone in the company had this great energy around this desire to be more successful and provide a very high level of service to customers, but we weren't allowing them to do that. So once we started tapping into that, it was easy to get momentum and energy and enthusiasm behind it".

To understand how Acklands-Grainger aligned its culture to become a driver of performance, you need to understand a bit more about the business it's in and how it operates.

As we read in Chapter 3, Acklands-Grainger is Canada's largest distributor of industrial, safety, and fastener products (and a subsidiary of Lake Forest, Illinois–based Grainger, the largest industrial distributor in the United States). It offers the largest collection of in-stock brand-name products and the largest number of exclusive private-label offerings in the industry. Overall, it is a single-source solution for more than 120,000 in-stock products, most of which are available through its mammoth 3,040-page catalogue.[1]

So what does that mean for its sales force, or, as Carruthers calls them, its team members?

"The product we sell is largely a commodity, and it's a very high-transaction business", says Carruthers, who became senior vice president of Grainger in 2007 and president of Grainger International in 2009. "We're competing against thousands of generally smaller competitors, so this tends to be a hand-to-hand-combat-type business. So a lot of the way you win in a transaction-intensive business is by having the best players and having them highly motivated to go that extra inch for the customer, and that's usually what allows you to be successful".

Thus began the journey in 2006—to motivate team members and to align their interests with those of the organization. The end result? Over the next 24 months, the business grew by more than $100 million, while profits tripled.[2]

How did the company do it?

"At the end of 2006, we brought the top 100 leaders together, we restructured the business and put a lot more power and autonomy into the hands of the people that serve the customer, and then for the first time in 2007, we brought together all of our local managers and presented a very clear vision", Carruthers said.

Carruthers says that part of that process involved looking at other leading organizations—like Shoppers Drug Mart, Wal-Mart, and Tim Hortons—going back into their respective histories, and seeing how they made the transition from relatively small players 10, 20, or even 30 years ago to the market leaders that they are today.

"We went back and told these stories, and then we said, look, in this market, this is us", said Carruthers. "We have this potential to really be a true market leader, and in order to do that, there are some very key things that we need to do, and those are orient ourselves around the customer and orient ourselves around our people, because that's how we're going to win. We used those case studies as analogies in terms of how we go after that".

As we know from earlier chapters, also key to the culture change was the introduction of a simple, yet comprehensive set of operating principles that became the basis of all decisions and of everything that Acklands-Grainger does as an organization. With some slight changes, the operating principles—customer focus, people focus, winning attitude, urgency and simplicity, and living the values—have become performance drivers for the entire Grainger organization worldwide.

The key to the operating principles, for Carruthers, is their simplicity:

"Simplicity is the key. I think people try to have 50 forums, a 50-slide PowerPoint deck, 20 hours of training, and so on", said Carruthers. "I think what makes things work is when they're really simple, consistent, straightforward, and easily understood. What I've always said is that you should be able to explain it to your child, and that to me is a test of whether or not it's simple".

As we also read earlier, the five principles—and their associated behaviours—outlined in what is now called the performance drivers, is what employees are measured on in their reviews (they receive a numerical ranking on each of the five).

"Repetition and actually using them every day and making sure they're always used, I think, was the key to embedding them", said Carruthers. "And I think there's been lots of work since then to keep driving them forward".

Equally as important to Carruthers in developing the operating principles as a tool for changing and aligning culture at Acklands-Grainger was tying those principles into a higher purpose. The two things together proved to be very powerful.

"To capture people's hearts and minds, it's really not enough to say we're going to be the biggest seller of hammers and toilet paper. That's not that exciting", Carruthers admitted.

"We have lots of great stories on a weekly basis, of how we've helped in emergencies, how we've saved lives, how we get businesses back up and running, how we keep troops and police and firefighters safe—if we start telling those stories and really make it clear that what we do makes an important difference in the economy and the lives of Canadians, that really starts to pull people's hearts and minds into it", he added.

What impact have these changes in the culture at Acklands-Grainger had on the performance of the organization?

"We had the best quarter in the history of the company in the first quarter of 2011. We made more money in the first quarter this year than in all of 2006; 30 percent more than that entire year. The end of that year was when we started our journey", said Carruthers.

Sean O'Brien, the president of Acklands Grainger Inc., told me that the organization's first-quarter results in 2011 showed revenue growth of 18 percent. Profits improved more than 300 percent.

"The alignment and the tools we're using are working", said O'Brien. "We're at infancy stage in terms of what we can really do. I truly believe that".

The Basis for Implementing Change

Organizational change—specifically, changing a culture—requires a lot of things to happen in alignment. And for that reason, it's a challenging process—even difficult. When you're trying to change the core behaviours within your organization, it takes an enormous focus. A lot of things have to go right. Change also takes time. In our business, I think we're often very concerned when clients want to see change happen fast. With respect to organizational culture, it doesn't work that way.

Before anything else happens, leaders first need to determine if they're ready to make a change. Yes, the desire to be in a better place, performance-wise, should be greater than the desire to maintain the status quo. But more than that, if leaders want to change the culture, they have to be prepared to also make the necessary changes to people, systems, and processes. And this is why the case of Acklands-Grainger is such a great example of how culture change can work: the change was strategic, it came from the top, and it was applied to people, systems, and processes. What's also so relevant about the Acklands-Grainger case is the objective measured against the end goal: Court Carruthers wasn't trying to tear everything down and start over. He saw the organization as a sleeping giant, and he saw culture as the tool to wake it. Key strategic changes, a handful of them (as in, the few and the mighty), were implemented to align that culture. And wow, just look at the results of those focused efforts on performance over time.

Change—if you go back to our discussion in Chapter 6 about motor skills and how the brain works—can be painful. There will be things that feel wrong, and that you're going to have to convince yourself are right. It's like Olympian Johann Olav Koss, now the president and CEO of

Right to Play, and his story of failure five weeks before the 1994 Winter Olympics in Lillehammer: he raced poorly in his practice runs, thought he was out of it, and realized that he had to focus on the things he was doing right. He also realized through his coach that he had to do some things differently, and those changes—like taking a turn a certain way—felt absolutely wrong to him. But they were in fact right. Effectively, in order to win, he had to unlearn and relearn what he had to do. Three gold medals in men's speed skating in Lillehammer (to add to his two other medals from Albertville in 1992) were the result.

Edgar Schein talks about this phenomenon—learning, unlearning, and relearning—in his well-known work *The Corporate Culture Survival Guide*. He also talks about how an organization should never start with the idea of culture change. Instead, it should start with the issues it is facing as an organization and then ask itself whether the current culture will help or hinder it in overcoming these issues. From there, Schein argues that the organization should build on cultural strengths and enable new behaviour by focusing on those strengths (and not on the weaknesses).[3]

I think Schein has identified a key point: leaders first have to look at their business challenges, understand those challenges, and then ask themselves what they need to do to enable the culture to evolve to overcome those challenges. They then have to create a vision of the future that enables a desire for change. Mission, vision, and values—these all provide the framework for assessment and evaluation of your current culture, but you also need a picture of your desired future. What do you want for your organization's future? Your values and your mission and vision should support that picture.

From there, structure your systems—people, training, resources, rewards and recognition, and so on—to align with that picture and reinforce the change. And then repeat, repeat, repeat. It takes 13 days to develop a new habit, but that's only for one behaviour. When you're talking about culture change, you're talking about changing a series of behaviours. When an organization's culture is already established and cultural change is on the horizon, people have to unlearn old values and change their current assumptions. More important, they have to want to be able to change their existing behaviours before they can take on new ones.

What are the things you're going to build from?

Changing the Culture at Yellow Media

We've talked about Yellow Media, a leading Internet, performance media, and marketing solutions company, at different points in the book. One of the more remarkable aspects of this organization, however, is the story of its culture change, which began back in 2002, after one of the most important leveraged buyouts in Canadian history took place.

As a refresher, what emerged from that buyout was that Yellow Pages Group (or YPG, one of the three companies in the Yellow Media network) became an independent company and, in 2003, completed an IPO.

YPG has undergone both massive growth and corporate structural changes over the past decade. Most recently, in late 2010, it converted from an income trust to a corporation.[4] The newly minted parent company, Yellow Media Inc., employs 4,100 people under its premium brands Trader Corporation, Canpages, and of course, YPG.

Marc Tellier is the president and CEO of YPG and CEO of both Trader and Canpages. Known for being a key player in the expansion and transformation of the Canadian communications and media industries, Tellier is also a prime example of the critical role that a leader plays in influencing the culture of an organization.

Tellier started his career at Bell Canada in 1990, and over the next 10 years moved up the corporate ladder, becoming senior vice president of partnership development and overseeing the launch of the first telco commercial high-speed Internet service in North America. After becoming president and CEO of Sympatico Lycos, Tellier moved to Bell Acti-Media[5] (which is the company that was acquired in the buyout referred to earlier). With the buyout and the IPO completed by 2003, YPG then undertook a comprehensive review of its corporate culture—and Tellier led the charge.

As we discussed earlier, when YPG became an independent company, Tellier inherited the culture that already existed at Bell ActiMedia. It was a culture that he describes as one of self-entitlement, where tenure ruled the day and defeat was easily accepted. In Tellier's view, the culture was both misunderstood and miscommunicated.

Although Tellier's career with the company began in the 1990s, YPG's roots go all the way back to the beginning of the twentieth century.

In fact, the organization published its first directory in 1908 and operated as a division of Bell Canada until 1971, when it was incorporated as Tele-Direct (Publications) Inc. (which was renamed Bell ActiMedia Inc. in 1999).[6]

In other words, Tellier was at the helm of an organization with a long history—and with solidly entrenched values and behaviours. His challenge was no small feat: to rebuild the culture at a company that was in essence a "100-year-old start-up", a term that Tellier often uses to describe YPG.[7]

His first step in 2003? To define YPG's culture moving forward.

"There were eight of us, and we literally locked ourselves inside a room for half a day", Tellier told our audience at the Corporate Culture Summit in 2010. "From the time we said, 'Let's define our corporate values' to when we rolled it out on the back of people's employee IDs was probably about five weeks. It was one of those things where you know you've just got to get it done".

As Tellier told me in a later conversation: "We weren't looking for culprits. We weren't looking for skeletons. We weren't looking to assign blame. We were looking to transform and improve. We felt the best way to drive the transformation was making sure we had a culture that was a set of values that was well understood." In the case of YPG, what emerged from Marc Tellier's locked-door meeting back in 2003 was a list of six core values for the organization: customer focus, competing to win, teamwork, passion, respect, and open and honest communication. Tellier and his team then decided that the next step in the process was to market those values (or ground rules) internally to employees. The best way? Have a few key disciples spread the word to the workforce.

"We thought, if this is going to work, it has to resonate with people", said Tellier. "So we found ambassadors, took those six values, and 'socialized' them through different parts of the business—sales, IT, production, and the various departments. We rolled it out that way so it felt very collaborative".

Tellier also says that in the years since the values were introduced, there's been only one change: "customer first" has replaced "customer focus" because of a need to match the YPG's values with the company's internal customer relationship management (CRM) platform.

At the end of the day, what impact has all of this focus on corporate culture had on the business? Does Tellier attribute YPG's success to its corporate culture?

"I'm in my tenth year at Yellow Pages, and when we sold the business on November 29, 2002, on a normalized basis, we had $291 million in EBITDA [earnings before interest, taxes, depreciation, and amortization]", Tellier told me last October. "Last year, we did almost $900 million in EBITDA. We've essentially tripled our revenue and tripled our EBITDA in nine years. So the focus was on transformation in an industry that more recently is also having to transform itself. We pretty much lead our industry globally on most operational or financial metrics. But there's always room for improvement".

"Culture will drive your performance", he added. "I could use endless sports analogies, but if you don't have a healthy dynamic in any locker room, you're dead. You might win sometimes, but you're not going to win consistently. Culture is a precursor to success".

Remember what our Canadian Corporate Culture Study revealed: 92 percent of respondents felt that leadership has the number one impact on corporate culture. Along those lines, and in my view, I think it's fair to say that the culture would not have changed at YPG if it hadn't been for Marc Tellier.

Says Tellier: "We've always been able to drive the change we've wanted to drive because we walk the talk. We're not going to waver and change our minds halfway through; that's not the way we operate. I think that framework is instilled in the corporate culture at YPG. When you make a commitment, you've got to follow up on it; you've got to live it by example".

Creating Organizational Change

To create organizational change and to change culture, here, in my view, are some of the most important elements.

The 10 Elements of Culture Change

- Leadership support (tone from the top)
- Communication
- Training
- Values and belief statements (credos)
- An aligned work structure
- Aligned systems
- Symmetry between the leadership and the desired culture
- A talent for integration and promotion of top performers
- An ability to make tough decisions to support the new culture
- Time

1. Leadership Support (Tone from the Top)

Change has to start from the top. Successful leaders drive and secure support for cultural change, and not just through verbal support. It's the proverbial "walk the talk". This is why so often, in order to change culture, a board decides to change the CEO or the CEO decides to change some of the other leaders. For some people, culture change is too hard to do. They can't see themselves living or behaving differently, or they feel that doing so would be disingenuous. The reality is that they're just not prepared. That picture of where the leader wants to take the organization isn't strong enough for them. And that's why you often see people come in from the outside, because without executive support, it's not going to happen. Leaders have to lead and live the change through their own behaviours, because, as we know through our study results, they are the number one influencer of culture.

In 2002, Tellier, a young, digitally savvy leader with strong business acumen, was given the reins at YPG. He was allowed to bring in seven new vice presidents, promote one director to a vice president, and keep one of his vice presidents. Why? Because substantial culture change was the end goal. The desire was to move away from the parochial telco mentality, to create a stand-alone business that could grow and build the directories business, digitally and otherwise. Tellier's leadership, and the vision he was selling, was seen as a key element of that process.

2. Communication

Communicating critical information about culture change, about the processes that support it, and about where and how it will succeed is really important. This is why WestJet's Culture Connection sessions work so well. Even though the organization is in its sixteenth year of business, WestJet still puts a heavy emphasis on the importance of these quarterly get-togethers between WestJetters and the organization's executive. The goal is to talk about the latest business updates, share daily stories, and otherwise communicate and reinforce the airline's culture. Hunter Camps at CN were an equally clever way to communicate culture and culture change. These two-day-long sessions brought together the organization's leaders from every function at CN. Attendees listened to and interacted with Hunter Harrison, and talked about culture change and the impact of the organization's guiding principles. Like the Culture Connection sessions, the camps operated to communicate and reinforce culture to frontline people. Both are opportunities for the executive team to hear about issues, and to see whether the culture is working or not. Both are driven from the top, and that's why they work.

3. Training

Training, as we've read, depends on behavioural change. It's not unlike the situation facing Johann Koss, who had to learn that even if some things feel wrong, they are actually right. That's the type of mindset you have to instil within your organization. It's important that people within the company be committed to the new behaviour, and an organization must help define that behaviour and train them in that way.

If your organization's new values, and the core behaviours associated with those new values, are different from what existed before, it will be critical to put support mechanisms in place. When you train a golf swing or when you train in anything, you don't just go out and play the game. You need techniques, coaching, and tools to help you form a new swing plane, for example. So if new behaviours are planned for your organization in order to drive cultural change, the leaders will have to set the tone, but they will also have to create systems to support it. And we're not just talking about basic training programs; this is about systems support.

For instance, one of the key things that Acklands-Grainger did in building a more customer-focused organization was the creation of its annual national sales and service conference. As you recall, this event was originally created in 2006, when 100 of the organization's leaders were brought together to talk about what they could do to make Acklands-Grainger more customer-focused. This is now a massive four-day-long event, part trade show, part conference, and part celebration, that brings together thousands of Acklands-Grainger leaders, salespeople, and suppliers. But it continues to be an event that's making Acklands-Grainger more customer-focused; this event is now part of the system and serves as a training tool to further reinforce the organization's customer-focused mentality. It supports the behaviours that Acklands-Grainger wants to encourage and communicate, and in that way, it works brilliantly.

4. Values and Belief Statements (Credos)

Creating values and belief statements for your organization is a key element of creating and reinforcing cultural change. This might involve creating focus groups by department and by region in order to understand what the existing values within the organization are or to determine which behaviours are healthy and strong and which need to change. Linking those findings to either a credo, a belief statement, or a vision or mission is key. It's also important to link those statements, if you can, to history or to aspects of the organization that are already a strength or a strong sentiment. It's almost impossible to start brand-new with something that doesn't exist. Do your research—marketing research: talk to customers or employees—to find out exactly what those things are. It's a very useful exercise that can provide a common understanding of the desired culture. It also reflects the actions that people will need to commit to on a day-to-day basis.

5. An Aligned Work Structure

Changing the physical structure of the company to align it with the desired culture may be necessary. For instance, Right to Play, which is now 10 years old, previously had both an executive leadership team and a leadership team. The levels were created so that the dissemination of information could flow down to the right people. It also seemed to make sense at the time because the company was expanding into 20 countries. But the structure didn't support the culture. The company realized that its structure was too big for the size of the organization, so it flattened out the structure and created one team.

6. Aligned Systems

Another key element of culture change is ensuring that your systems reflect your objectives. Ensure that your rewards and recognition are aligned with the behaviours that you're trying to support. Ask yourself this: if you're not rewarding the behaviours that you want to support and/or recognizing people for those behaviours, what are you recognizing and rewarding? Probably the wrong things or the things that were recognized in the past. This is often a difficult process because people get used to the way they've historically been compensated. Also, review all of your organization's work systems: how people are promoted, how managers interact and work together, and how employees formally and informally solve issues. In order to do this, perform frequent assessments, perhaps annually (biannually at a minimum), by geography, region, division, and department to find out where people are in terms of the culture change. Review your executives' behaviour as a starting point, to ensure that they are really living those values. This is absolutely critical.

7. Symmetry between the Leadership and the Desired Culture

Look for incongruences between your leadership and your desired culture. If someone is flying the wrong way—and this might happen over time—this has to be corrected quickly or changed. Assess the situation, and then change it or alter it as required. Remember that good behaviour should be rewarded and reinforced.

8. A Talent for Integration and Promotion of Top Performers

Be great at integrating new people into the organization and promoting the top ones.

9. An Ability to Make Tough Decisions to Support the New Culture

To support cultural change, leaders will sometimes need to make uncomfortable decisions. But making those decisions is critical. A great example again is from the Atlanta Falcons: current general manager Thomas Dimitroff's decision to let quarterback Michael Vick go. This was a big decision, given that Vick was the star. But in Dimitroff's mind, he wasn't aligned with the team's values, so the decision had to be made to support the culture and the overall behaviours that he wanted to see in the team. It was a very tough decision, but it was the right one to make.

10. Time

An old boss of mine used to say: if you want to change culture, start by changing the colour of the walls. He was talking about the importance of putting your own stamp on an organization, but the point he was trying to make was that change shouldn't be implemented just for the sake of being able to say that you changed things. The walls are a starting point—changing people and systems takes time.

John Crocker of HOOPP, the Healthcare of Ontario Pension Plan, realized this when he became president and CEO of the organization in 2001. We've read about HOOPP, one of the largest and most successful pension plans in Canada—which provides a defined-benefit pension plan to 260,000 of Ontario's hospital and community-based health-care workers—and its incredible performance despite the overall global trend towards pension shortfalls.

When Crocker first started with the organization in the 1990s, the opportunities for culture change were plainly evident.

"It was very insular and totally running below the radar", Crocker told me, speaking of the culture of the organization when he first came on board as chief investment officer in 1998. "The place was really two operations—the administration of the pension plan and the money management group. It was a very paternalistic kind of place, an entitlement kind of place. I characterize it as a small-town Ontario family not really realizing that it was a multibillion-dollar operation".

Crocker implemented one of the most step-focused cultural changes that I've ever seen. He recognized that in order to do phenomenal investment work, you also had to be great at pension administration—and in order to do that, you had to develop best-in-class people and systems. He kept upgrading the team and developing it over time. Crocker also recognized that if the investment group and the administrators were like oil and water, he couldn't force them together. Instead, he had to figure out a way to align their interests and unify them under a single-minded purpose, which he did through the creation of the organization's rallying cry, "delivering on the pension promise".

"People think we're doing God's work here", Crocker told me. "We have one client. We all understand what the objectives are. We're a long-term investor. The people here are all members of the plan, and I think they take pride not just in doing a good job, but in a social sense—in that there are 260,000 people out there who are relying on us for their financial future".

What Crocker did to the culture at HOOPP was thoughtful and strategic. In many ways he typifies the Level 5 leader as described by author Jim Collins in his bestseller *Good to Great*.

Level 5 leaders:

"Embody a paradoxical mix of personal humility and professional will".

"Display a workman like diligence—more plow horse than show horse".

and

"Are fanatically driven, infected with an incurable need to pro-duced sustained results".[8]

The results at HOOPP, as we read earlier, speak for themselves. Pensions plans in general are in shortfall, particularly following the reces-sion. But HOOPP emerged from 2009 fully funded—in fact, it was 102 percent funded, with $31.1 billion in net assets available for benefits (an increase of $4.4 billion over the previous year). The performance trend continues: in 2010, the fund was valued at more than $35.7 billion.

HOOPP's culture set the stage for this performance. And for that I credit Crocker and his team. Someone else will now be coming in to take the reins when Crocker retires at the end of 2011. HOOPP is set up for success, but it took time and it took an understanding of what the com-pany's core values and beliefs were. Changing organizational culture requires leadership commitment and proper execution. It also requires time. But it can be done.

Chapter 12

The Culture Club:
The Importance of
Culture Champions

If your actions inspire others to dream more, learn more,
do more and become more, you are a leader.

—JOHN QUINCY ADAMS

THE MAIN CHAMPION of culture is the leader. But in any organization that is looking to either change or otherwise continuously improve its culture, it is crucial for the leader to identify at an early stage who else within the organization is going to be on his side. Cultural change takes enormous commitment from the leaders of an organization, but it also requires other champions who will connect to the bigger picture. It's critical that these individuals be found, and the entire executive team should be behind this and actively searching.

What are culture champions? They're people who have the desired behaviours of the culture that the company aspires to and who are visible within the organization. Leaders need to look for champions at all levels, and this can be done by creating all sorts of interfaces with people at various levels of the organization. Champions either are in leadership roles or take a leadership position—and there's a difference here that's worth pointing out. We define leadership in our business as followership, in the sense that leaders are people whom others follow, or they are individuals who have an impact through others. Champions may not necessarily be on a senior leadership team, but they have the desired behaviours and they make themselves visible. It takes a certain amount of natural persuasion and charisma to encourage change in others—you may or may not find this in your culture champions, as they may not all be extroverts, but they have bought in.

When you find your champions, it's important that you put them in positions where they have the opportunity to show examples of the ways in which they're living and supporting the culture—and then reward them for that behaviour. Why? Because other people in the organization will notice this; they're going to notice that the behaviour is being recognized, and they're going to start to emulate that behaviour. It's human nature in many ways: we follow the people who are being rewarded for exhibiting certain types of behaviours.

When I think of champions and their importance, I think back to Hunter Harrison's story (which we talked about earlier in the book) of the star IT manager whom he discovered at one of his Hunter Camps. She had skill, intelligence, and business acumen—exactly the kind of leader that Harrison wanted to develop at CN. When he found out that there was no specific plan for her (beyond having her sit around for six or seven years waiting for her boss to retire), he created a position for her. The story emphasizes the importance of not only unearthing talent but also discovering champions.

"If you find good leaders, if you find even further what I call champions, don't lose them", Harrison told our audience at our breakfast series back in June 2010. "Too many of us in the business of leading people don't recognize champions. We discovered champions at CN, and we did everything we could to help, support, and motivate them to change the leadership in the company".

Characteristics of Culture Champions

What are the key characteristics of culture champions? Here are a few to help you identify these champions within your own organization.

1. *Culture champions are energetic and supportive of the change.* More than anything, champions have great enthusiasm for the change; they believe it is the right thing to do. They may not always be extroverted people, but they do have to have the ability to be persuasive—through their words and their actions, but ideally through the latter. If you've identified someone as a potential champion and you have to draw out her support for the change, than she is probably not the right person.

2. *Culture champions have natural credibility and leadership skills.* Others follow these individuals. They get results. If they're not in direct leadership roles, they achieve results through others—through collaboration, or simply by getting things done. What you are looking for in your champions is people who will be living examples of your organization's values.

3. *Culture champions have the ability to communicate the need for change.* Culture champions have the ability to articulate why there is a need for change. When they come across someone who is not moving in the right direction, they can explain why it's so important that she change course. They understand the critical importance of buy-in across the board.

4. *Culture champions are empathetic and appreciate how difficult change can be.* Champions don't expect change to take place overnight. They may be enthusiastic, but they also understand that just because they're charging forward with culture change, this doesn't mean that others will be able to do so as easily. Culture champions understand that it's more difficult for some people. If it reaches the stage where a person has to be moved out because he can't adapt to the change, a culture champion will still have empathy and understanding.

5. *Culture champions have the ability to make tough decisions.* They can make tough decisions about their own behaviour and tough decisions about the behaviour of others. Culture champions are also not afraid to communicate with the leadership when they see a repeated instance of someone not living the values.

6. *Culture champions should be living examples of the values.* Culture champions should exhibit repeated examples of their successful use

of the desired behaviours in the new environment. They should be consistently showing others these behaviours on a day-to-day basis.

Supporting Your Champions

How do you enable your champions within your organization? Part of it is monitoring. That can be accomplished through a cultural assessment and by identifying where the issues are. If there are gaps in certain departments, for instance, leaders in that area should be made aware of those gaps and be encouraged to put more champions in place so that they can address the issues.

Your systems also have to support your champions. They should be reviewed regularly to ensure that they're supporting the current-day culture and not the past.

For instance, we talked about the importance of changing performance management systems so that they measure behaviour. This is what Maple Leaf Foods, Yellow Media, Agrium, TELUS, and Acklands-Grainger, to name a few, have done, and it's what more and more organizations are starting to do. The fact is that if you're not measuring people on how they're acting, you're probably doing a lot of things right and a major thing wrong.

Organizations should also consider other systems designed to reinforce behaviour and find new ways for the people in your organization to engage. It could be something as innovative as your organization's own version of a Hunter Camp. Or perhaps it's developing a regular way to get people together to talk about culture, like WestJet's Culture Connection sessions. The important thing is to build a regular event or system that reinforces the behaviours. Doing so provides fertile ground for existing culture champions to flourish, or for new champions to emerge.

Remember at all times that people drive behaviour change in an organization—not business plans, not even systems. These things support the change, but it's people, your champions, that drive it. By recognizing and rewarding these individuals for their behaviours and for living the values, you're reinforcing the culture—either the new culture or the culture that you're looking to continuously grow.

Champions are the people who are going to drive the cause for cultural change. You should still be the biggest cheerleader (because if you're not living the change, how can you ask anyone else to?). Culture is so deep; it's so rooted in behaviour. If as a leader you're not managing culture, it won't be long before it's managing you.

Chapter 13

Culture Clash: Why Culture Is a Critical Component of International Expansion

---

The thing I have learned at IBM is that culture is everything.

—LOUIS V. GERSTNER JR. (FORMER CEO OF IBM)

EACH FEBRUARY, our firm hosts an event called the Corporate Culture Summit. We bring together a few hundred leaders and their executive teams from our Canada's 10 Most Admired Corporate Cultures program to talk about the latest issues in corporate culture. The Canada's 10 annual gala usually follows the summit, so it's a good excuse to get everyone together.

This year, because of some of the organizations that we knew would be in attendance, we decided to put together a panel called "The Power of Culture in International Growth". Executives from four organizations (Roger Hardy, co-founder, president, and CEO of Coastal Contacts; Court Carruthers, president of Grainger International; Herb Singer, founder, president, and CEO of Discount Car and Truck Rentals Ltd.; and Carolyn Clark, senior vice president, human resources of Fairmont Hotels & Resorts) formed the basis of this powerhouse panel. Up for discussion was how they've extended the reach of their organization's culture on an international level, and how to turn culture into an arsenal for expansion and growth.

One of the more memorable stories from the panel came from Court Carruthers, and, much to everyone's surprise and delight, the story centered around his attempts at Bollywood dancing.

Carruthers is responsible for all of Grainger's business outside of the United States, which amounts to approximately 20 percent of the company's sales. Because of Illinois-based Grainger's expansion into India, Carruthers was in attendance at the company's annual national meeting in Mumbai in January. Part of the meeting involved a ballroom dance-off with 150 team members (who were apparently insistent that Carruthers take part in the performance).

"They had practiced for months every single day with choreographers; seven- and eight-minute Bollywood dance numbers. So of course, they wanted me to do the same, and I ended up on stage", Carruthers told our audience. As funny as his story was, there was a message in it from Carruthers: "If you're not comfortable doing things differently everywhere you operate, it can be very challenging. 'When in Rome, do as the Romans do': it's absolutely essential in terms of making everybody comfortable and to build your culture globally".

Our audience learned quite a bit from this session, and so did we. What the panel revealed more than anything else is the importance of transporting your culture abroad and how critically important it is to do it right.

In Chapter 10, we showed that mergers and acquisitions can be a culture killer. That is, without a thoughtful assessment of the acquired culture, without a long, hard look at culture differences between the acquiring and the acquired company, and without any serious consideration of what your organization is adopting and/or what it is willing and not willing to tolerate on the culture front, M&As can have a serious impact on your organization's culture.

In this chapter, we're going to look at the impact of culture on international expansion in more detail. Through a "lessons learned" approach, we'll examine how different organizations have taken their culture abroad and what words of wisdom they have to pass along.

Transporting your organization's culture around the world is an exciting prospect. But deciding how best to do it often has to be learned through experience—and sometimes by trial and error. The organizations that have done it well have steadfastly relied on the guiding principles of their own domestic corporate cultures as a starting point, understanding full well that without an appreciation of the local cultures and markets that they're doing business in, they simply won't succeed.

Culture Carriers

Carolyn Clark, the senior vice president of human resources for Fairmont Hotels & Resorts, knows firsthand the challenges—and rewards—of transporting culture on a global scale, and she had several key messages to pass along to our audience at the summit.

Canadians will remember the Fairmont brand as Canadian Pacific Hotels, a 100-year-old organization that merged with the U.S.-based Fairmont in 2000. The freshly rebranded Fairmont Hotels & Resorts began its international expansion in earnest in 2003, and now has 64 properties, with 30,000 employees, in 18 different countries around the world.[1]

As Clark explained to our Corporate Culture Summit audience, Fairmont Hotels & Resorts has recently expanded into new markets, with three new hotels in China and also properties in the Middle East and Africa.

The hotel's first foray into a market outside of North America was in Dubai. And for Clark, the experience honed her philosophy with respect to international expansion, especially when it comes to corporate culture: be persistent when replicating your culture on a global scale. Be responsive to local concerns and respectful of the local culture and values, yes, but despite the obstacles, stay true to what made your organization's culture so successful in the first place.

"We had never operated a hotel in the Middle East before, so it was all brand-new", Clark told our audience. "It was very important to us that we apply the management practices that are integral to our culture and to our success internationally".

Focusing on one of the organization's core brand promises, warm and engaging service, those management practices are based on Fairmont's concept of "Service Plus", a comprehensive HR platform that embodies the organization's philosophy to select the best, lead with the best, train and develop, and recognize and reward.

Included in the Service Plus concept is a nonnegotiable structured interview for all new applicants.

But when Clark met with recruitment agencies in Dubai, she ran into a few brick walls.

"We quickly learned that no one who works in Dubai actually lives in Dubai, and that we would have to go to 10 different countries to hire 600 colleagues", said Clark. "We said to the recruitment agencies that all of our colleagues need to speak English, and they said, 'No, that'll never happen'. Then when we talked about our structured interview, they said, 'No, that'll never happen'. And we said yes—we will make it happen".

Fairmont Hotels & Resorts' international hiring ratio is 1:20 or 1:25, and in the case of Dubai, the company stayed true to that ratio. Clark says that the recruiters went to 10 different countries and handpicked every single employee to ensure that they all met the organization's service requirement. Furthermore, the experience set the reputation for the organization's hotels internationally.

"It's an incredible story because of the rigour we thought was so important to apply", said Clark. "Because of the success we had there, we were able to expand in the Middle East. And because we did it differently than other hotels in Dubai, in terms of how we treat people, we very quickly became an employer of choice".

Her advice to our audience was this: "When you're opening internationally, stay true to what you believe is core to your corporate culture and to your success, and try to replicate that internationally."

Dealing with Cultural Differences

We talked about Coastal Contacts, the world's largest online retailer of eyeglasses and contact lenses, in Chapter 5, discussing how it does a great job of communicating its culture to its customers. The company has also become very knowledgeable about international expansion over the past few years. Although founded by Roger Hardy in Vancouver in 2000, Coastal has been expanding globally over the past decade. About 40 percent of the company's business now comes from outside of North America—from Europe, Asia, Australia, and New Zealand. In fact, Coastal now services customers in more than 150 countries through its family of websites, which include CoastalContacts.com, ClearlyContacts.ca, Lensway.co.uk, ClearlyContacts.com.au, Yasuilens.com, Maxlens.com, and Coastallens.com.[2]

Coastal tapped into both the consumer's desire to shop online for anything (even glasses and contacts) and the realization that selling these products online meant lower prices. Who knew that you could sit at home in your pyjamas and order a pair of glasses off the Internet at a cost far lower than the traditional brick-and-mortar model of eyewear purchasing? The company's growth has been significant: in one week in March 2011, for instance, it reported a record eyeglasses order of approximately $2.0 million USD (or 28,000 pairs of eyeglasses).[3]

Hardy and his team began to expand outside of Canada in 2004, buying a business in Stockholm, Sweden, primarily to service the company's European markets.

The expansion plans were ambitious, but they were not without a few cultural hiccups along the way.

"In terms of challenges, the cultural nuances are one of the key things we've run into", Hardy told our audience at the summit.

Hardy noted that the members of his team had to get used to the way their Swedish counterparts conducted meetings. In Sweden, after a point is made in a meeting, Hardy said, it's customary for there to be a three- to five-second pause, during which the person receiving the message is meant to internalize and think about the comment. For Canadians, Hardy said, the tendency is to jump on a point and respond immediately—a trait that can be perceived by Swedes as not listening.

"One side thinks the meeting is really productive—'Wow, we're really making progress'—and the other side says, 'No one's listening to me'", said Hardy.

"We were walking out of our meetings for the first four or five months of that acquisition thinking, 'We're really moving the ball forward", he added. "And they were walking out of the room thinking, 'These Canadians never shut up; they don't listen'. Soon after that, a consultant came in and translated Swedish to English cultures. It was so valuable".

Hardy says that when Coastal bought the Swedish business in 2004, it was a $20 million operation, and it is now about an $80 million operation.

"I don't think we would've had that success if we hadn't realized early on that we needed to get everyone on the same page, for those differences to be aligned", Hardy advised our audience. "We learned that there are national cultural differences, as opposed to company cultural differences".

Understand and Be Understood

For Carolyn Clark of Fairmont, transporting your culture around the world successfully involves a simple concept: seek first to understand and then to be understood. In other words, try to understand the local culture, markets, and employment practices, but at the same time, remember that the true competitive advantage lies with those that can replicate their own culture in the new environment.

This is a tricky balancing act, one that is perfected only through experience—and through trial and error. And also through something that Clark calls "culture carriers".

Consider Fairmont's foray into China. When the organization was opening hotels in both Shanghai and Beijing a few years ago, Clark and her team were advised to hire local directors of human resources—who would presumably know the local employment market—rather than sending in one of their own human resources leaders from Fairmont (that is, someone who was obviously well versed in Fairmont's culture, management, and HR practices). Based on that advice, Fairmont hired two local human resource directors—one in Shanghai and one in Beijing.

Both failed.

"While they understood the local culture, they had trouble adapting to our company culture", Clark told our audience. "So we sent over two of our own North American HR directors, and they are doing really well. We paired them with strong number twos who know the local culture. It was an interesting lesson".

Based on Fairmont's experience in China, and on its experience launching a new hotel in Jaipur, India (scheduled to open at the end of 2011), Clark passed along the following pieces of advice for how best to grow internationally while staying true to your organization's corporate culture:

- First, two years before you go, send a team into the new market to meet with the local competitors.
- Try to understand everything you can about the local market, culture, and employment practices.
- Identify what is true to your brand, to your organization's success, and to your culture, and try to replicate that in the new environment.
- Send in the culture carriers—your own organization's leaders; individuals who can teach your culture and inject your organization's DNA into the local team.
- Balance this in-house expertise with local expertise and a local management team.
- Defy the naysayers: if you're told it can't be done, believe that it can be.
- Stay true to your brand and stand by it.

While Clark believes in the concept of culture carriers, those individuals also need their own special training. In fact, Clark says that although the company did a good job teaching the Fairmont culture to its leaders in its new locations, it could have done a better job teaching its own leaders from North America.

"I'll use China as an example. Their protocol in meetings is entirely different than here in North America," said Clark, who noted that Fairmont is launching a new online training tool where employees can fill out a questionnaire on how they would make decisions in Canada or the United States. The tool would then mirror how those same decisions would be made in a country like India or China.

"You can see, going into new countries, the nuances you need to be mindful of. That's one of our lessons learned."

Grainger Keeps It Simple

For Carruthers, successful international expansion on the culture front is all about keeping it simple.

Carruthers describes the Grainger culture as one that has an aggressive focus on results, profitable growth, and market share. But it's also an organization with a unique family feeling, one that is highly committed to the community, to its customers, and to its suppliers.

How do you transport these ideals around the world?

"What's important is to keep it to a very small number of principles that you can actually explain, so that you can hire and manage and train and develop and reward people around something that's that simple".

Historically, Grainger has focused its business on the United States and Canada. In the last three to four years, however, Carruthers said, the company has become serious about international expansion, adding two to three countries a year, primarily in South America and the major Asia-Pacific economies. Starting this year, he told our audience, the goal is to ramp that up to five or six countries a year.

Carruthers said that the organization has had great success on the cultural side between its U.S. and Canadian offices—in other words, between Grainger and its Canadian subsidiary, Acklands-Grainger Inc. (AGI).

In fact, in its push to go international, Grainger turned to a set of principles developed at AGI, the Canadian office, as a guideline.

As we've read earlier, those operating principles (now used as performance drivers) are customer focus, people focus, winning attitude, urgency and simplicity, and living the values.

"We've used these principles as a basis for driving cultural consistency around the world", said Carruthers. "There are a number of elements that resonate with people regardless of cultural background. Keep the message simple—that doesn't mean it's generic—and it can be very simply explained in a way that really does transcend national boundaries".

Carruthers says that Grainger approaches international growth through a mix of greenfield investing and acquisition.

When it comes to making an acquisition, however, and to hiring locally, Carruthers has a litmus test—and it focuses on cultural fit.

"The question we always use, regardless of how good the business is or the financials look, is: would you hire the person who's going to be CEO?" Carruthers told our audience. "And if the answer to that is no, then we don't buy the company. We don't partner with the company. And that's a pretty tough test because it means we walk away from financially promising deals that we know aren't going to work down the road".

Carruthers has a slightly different take on hiring local management. Whereas Clark's strategy has focused on having a Fairmont person in an executive role with a local executive in a number two position, Carruthers takes the opposite approach.

For instance, he noted that it is his preference to hire a local CFO, but to have an expat (a senior-level Grainger employee) in the number two position, supporting the local person.

"I have a very strong bias to local everything", said Carruthers. "So we would tend to have one expat in business, generally a number two in finance. But we don't put them in as the CFO. We put them in as the number two. They're the conduit; they're a bit of a cultural link as well".

For Carruthers, a successful export of culture—at least for Grainger—involves thinking about it in the following terms: it's not about exporting a culture from North America; it's about building a global corporate culture.

"There's the warmth and the passion and the fun we have in our businesses in South America; the spectacle and the celebration, the teamwork that we have in our businesses in India and China and Japan. Those things are actually interesting elements of building a culture in other markets around the world, and we actually try to share that always—not just the importation of a culture from North America", said Carruthers.

The other major lesson Carruthers said he has learned? Be prepared to make mistakes. And a little humility goes a long way.

"Whatever you do, you will screw it up", said Carruthers. "I don't get it right all the time, but the process is actually more important than the output. The fact that you try, the fact that you care, the fact that you try and fix the mistakes, the fact that you try and do locally relevant. . . . The fact you're going to do the conference calls at 6 in the morning, at 10 at night, so it's convenient for them: that actually matters more than getting the output right all the time".

His final piece of advice to our audience? "As long as you're very open and you're focused on the process of trying to get it right, in my experience, there's a huge amount of forgiveness. That humility, that openness, that commitment to getting it right from a process perspective is very important".

The Process at Four Seasons

Kathleen Taylor is the president and CEO of Four Seasons Hotels and Resorts, with 34,000 employees. To her, when opening a new hotel, every situation—every market, every country, and every building—is unique. The same perspective is given to hiring, no matter where it takes place across the globe. There is a tried-and-true formula at Four Seasons for bringing the right people into the organization. Carrying out that process properly is critical to the organization's culture.

"This is the tipping point, if you will; this is the highest-risk moment in the spreading of the culture", Taylor told me as we sat down for an interview in her office in north Toronto in April of this year. "We do it a lot of different ways is the answer".

Take Baku, the capital of Azerbaijan, as a case in point. Four Seasons will open a new hotel in Baku in late 2011 (the organization's eighty-sixth property). Although Four Seasons operates in Eastern Europe, Eurasia, northern Africa, and the Middle East, this is its first foray into the Caucasus. To Taylor, one of the first steps when opening in a new market is to put the new hotel into very capable—and familiar—hands. This is typically accomplished through lateral transfers or promotions (in the case of Baku, it's the former, as the new general manager is the former head of Four Seasons Hotel Istanbul at Sultanahmet). Taylor says that the new general manager in Baku will form his senior leadership team by recruiting other people in the company who want to get a promotion into Baku. But he will also need to hire locally based individuals at that senior level.

"His preference would be to open the hotel with 100 percent Four Seasons transfers, but sometimes that's not possible", Taylor told me. "Language and local standards typically drive some of this. Sometimes you need a local for HR. Sometimes you need a local for finance. So you go out and try to find the people who look and feel and act and walk the talk like Four Seasons people, and you bring them in".

With the senior leadership team in place, the next step is a big one—hiring the rest of the staff. In the case of Baku, this means bringing 450 people on board. Again, lateral transfers and promotions are the first step. Taylor said that in the case of Baku, the Four Seasons expects that somewhere between 30 and 130 people will raise their hands. But every opening is different.

"When we opened in Dublin, we had 150 people transfer; when we opened in Las Vegas, we had 200. So these hotels got a real jump start. Baku is likely going to be tougher", said Taylor. "We opened the hotel in Milan with not one single internal transfer. No one would go. The Italians who had left Italy had no interest in returning, but they said, 'Look, I'll go for six weeks, I'll go for three months. I'll help out, but I am not going back to live there'".

In fact, whenever there is a shortage of internal transfers—whether because of a lack of interest, as was the case in Milan, or because of a lack of opportunity as a result of visa or other restrictions on importing labour—preopening support, provided by Four Seasons staff members from all over the world, becomes even more important.

To Taylor, moving Four Seasons people around the globe for these limited stints is an important element of the organization's career and leadership development programs. Like internal transfers and promotions, it's also a critical component in the successful transportation and reinforcement of the Four Seasons culture.

"The young housekeeper who goes or the room service waiter or the engineer—they've now experienced a completely different operation in a completely different cultural and environmental setting", said Taylor. "They bring all of that technical support, but they also bring the culture. They bring the attitude. They lead by example. They go back to their hotel, and then that cross-pollinates. That's the story, and that formula has worked".

Despite lateral transfers, promotions, and preopening support, what Taylor calls the "mass hire" still needs to take place. Again, the Four Seasons formula comes into play. Serious candidates are put through five separate interviews, and the organization hires for attitude and behaviour rather than skill—as Taylor says, once the right candidate is hired, "We then train for skill".

Once the tough task of hiring is complete, there's a myriad of other considerations—even when it comes to service.

"We have to change the cadence of service sometimes; we have to adjust our thinking around our service standards because they may or may not work in that location", says Taylor. "But there are dozens and dozens of Four Seasons people involved at all times in one of these openings. And it's quite extraordinary to see the energy and dedication that comes out of that".

Whatever ultimately happens when launching a Four Seasons hotel in a new market, finding the right people—especially at the leadership level—is critical.

"As good a job as we do of promotion from within, we can't grow all of our leaders from inside of the company, and some don't want to go, so we need to go and find people," said Taylor. "There's a different flavour each time we do it, which is one of the things that's kind of aggravating, but also energizing because there's a new learning experience every time. But the leader is key: miss the mark on the GM—it's over".

Agrium Goes Global

As we read in Chapter 3, Mike Wilson joined Agrium—a major retail supplier of agricultural products in North and South America and a leading global producer and marketer of agricultural nutrients and industrial products—as COO in 2000 (he became CEO in 2002). The Calgary-based company has a market cap of $15 billion.

At the beginning of the 2000s, Agrium had two business units—Wholesale and Retail—and a corporate group. The company's market cap was just under $1 billion. To Wilson, the wholesale unit and the corporate group, and their 1,200 combined employees, operated as one. As for Agrium's U.S.-based retail business, it had less than 1,000 employees and at the time made less than $1 billion in revenue (with approximately $60 to $70 million in EBITDA).[4]

"It got to the point where the board of directors and the corporation were thinking of selling it because it was sort of an orphan", Wilson told me over the phone from Calgary.

Fast-forward to the present: besides the growth in market cap, Agrium now has three business units: Wholesale, Retail, and Advanced Technologies. And what about the retail group, which the board once considered selling? In fiscal 2011, it is forecasted to bring in $8 to $9 billion in revenue, with an EBITDA of approximately $600 million.

So how do you get from a $1 billion market cap to a $15 billion market cap? First, in the case of Agrium, Wilson's leadership has been a driving force. Second, you look at culture: as we've seen in earlier chapters, Agrium put a much more concentrated focus on its corporate culture, implementing Formula for Success (as at Acklands-Grainger, five simple operating principles for employees to live by), a forced ranking system, a performance management system, key performance indicators, and other recognition and rewards programs. But to Wilson, the company's success can also be attributed to two key factors: diversification and growth— aggressive global growth.

"We're now in Argentina; we're expanding into Uruguay and Chile. We market heavily into Brazil. We made an acquisition in Europe. We just bought the Australian Wheat Board, and we're the largest retailer now in Australia. We have a joint venture in China. So the company is diversified globally, by product and by business", said Wilson.

So how does Agrium's culture get transported around the world?

Like the Four Seasons' Kathleen Taylor, Wilson sees people as the key to successful international expansion. But he's less likely to rely on internal transfers to achieve that goal.

"The peak of my experience has been, no matter where you go in the world, there are great people there; you just need to water them a little and bring them out—fertilize them a little", Wilson told me. "You don't need to put a bunch of expats in to do it".

"When we make an acquisition, we do a lot of work up front to try to understand the company we're acquiring—not just the financial results, but to try and get an understanding of what kind of culture they have. It's amazing how quickly people will latch on to our values and to the way we operate. For those that don't, we change them out, and we don't take two years to make that decision. You have to drive that change quickly", said Wilson.

Another key aspect of Agrium's success on the global stage, according to Wilson, is cultural fluency, meaning, that the company hires a team worldwide—and at the corporate head office in Calgary—that includes people with different nationalities and from different cultures. In other words, it hires individuals who can provide critical insight into international expansion and growth.

"Success to me is that cultural fluency", said Wilson. "We have Australians in our group. We have people who are from Norway or from Africa or from the Middle East. They recognize differences in values, and when we make an acquisition they say, 'Let me tell you [about] a few things you might run into'".

He added: "We're putting a lot of effort into diversity right now, but it's a long haul. We're trying to do everything we can to be positioned so that when a new immigrant comes to Canada who has an education that fits our needs, we don't go looking for them—they come looking for us".

Like Carruthers and Taylor, Wilson also appreciates that a North American view is sometimes your worst enemy when you are expanding abroad.

"I've seen so many people go in and blow it as they go into other regions of the world, assuming, 'I've got a model that works in North America, and that model is going to work in China or wherever in the world'", said Wilson. "What you need to do is understand how they think and how they act and then try to bring the better parts of their culture into yours, and what you'll find is that they'll want to work for you".

To Wilson, Agrium's success on the global expansion front will depend not only on its ability to transport its own culture successfully, but also on the ability of Agrium's people to drive that growth.

"If you look at where our company is going, we said by 2014 we'll be at a billion dollars in EBITDA from retail, which means that in a period of about 10 years, we'll take it up by a factor of 12," said Wilson.

"We will triple our footprint in North Africa; we will be in Central Europe; we'll be stronger in Western Europe; we will expand in Uruguay, Chile, and Brazil in a bigger way; we'll use our Australian footprint to move into Southeast Asia," he added. "You'll see a much more global company, so culturally we have to be able to be in those regions of the world, deliver value from a shareholder point of view, from a regional point of view, and it's all going to be done through people".

Conclusion

When organizations are expanding abroad, outside of their Canadian or U.S. markets, it's critical to consider culture in the equation. As Mike

Wilson said, many organizations make the mistake of walking in blind and assuming that whichever company they acquire or start up in a foreign market will simply adapt to the existing culture of the mother ship, so to speak. This is sometimes a fatal mistake.

Culture should be a consideration from the get-go—from the initial meetings where a potential partnership or acquisition is being discussed, and especially from the hiring stage. As we've seen through our examples, it's key for any organization, when expanding internationally, to ensure that the people who will represent its brand abroad understand and exhibit the key behaviours that define its culture.

There's a delicate balance between bringing in your own people to ensure that your culture is nurtured and grows on foreign soil, while at the same time appreciating local cultures in other markets and incorporating them in that process. The best of the best know that this can sometimes be a difficult dance and a never-ending moving target. Relying on your organization's own guiding principles is a starting point. So is doing some of the other things we've discussed, such as conducting a thoughtful and detailed cultural assessment. We often recommend this critical step to our clients when they are considering a merger or acquisition. Why? So that they know exactly what they are getting into, or at the very least know where the gaps are on the culture front, before anything is signed or agreed to. Culture can often be the "go, no-go" factor in a merger or acquisition, because what you're really getting in a transaction is the culture.

I'll leave the final piece of advice to Grainger's Court Carruthers: when you're expanding abroad, don't forget—a little humility goes a long way.

Chapter 14

Culture and Governance:
The Role of the Board in
Supporting Corporate Culture

Individual commitment to a group effort—that is
what makes a team work, a company work,
a society work, a civilization work.

—Vince Lombardi

In terms of governance, the role of the board is twofold: to support the CEO (which also entails hiring or firing the CEO, in a public company) and to help the CEO and the organization set a future direction. If culture is not factored into either of those two areas—that is, if the CEO that the board chooses is not right for the culture or if the direction from the board does not address culture (because it is simply not on the radar)—then I would argue that the board is not really doing its job.

But mine is not a common view. In fact, in anything you read on governance—any book, white paper, piece of business school research, or anything else—culture, in terms of the importance of the board's awareness and enforcement of it, will rarely be addressed. But organizations, as evidenced by some of the clients we work with, are starting to see the light. They're zeroing in on how important it is for any new or future board member to have culture on her radar screen.

151

For instance, in two of our recent board searches, culture was high on the agenda. In one instance, we were asked to find a director who would be a real cultural fit with the CEO—who would help mentor and partner with this individual and assist him in continuing to shape the culture of the organization. In the other search, a huge piece of the new director's role would be to help the CEO evolve the organization's culture and to continue to support it. What we're seeing is that at those organizations where culture is paramount, the board now has to play an important role in supporting those efforts.

Directors need to promote an organization's culture, and they need to recognize culture as an asset. In order to do these things, they need to have some level of access to the organization (all the while recognizing that there is a line between operations and governance).

A great example of how this can work is Maple Leaf Foods' Board Connect program.

Every year, the organization's independent board members spend a day with one of Maple Leaf Foods' top-performing employees—it may be the president of an operating company or a senior leader from one of the organization's businesses. The objective on each side? The employees of Maple Leaf get to tap into the experience of the independent board member. The director, on the other hand, has an opportunity to gain additional insights into the business and to engage with employees.[1] The overall point of Board Connect is to allow the two individuals to work together for a day and to provide an open flow of information.[2]

"What we did is we gathered experiences, and we'd say to the independent board members: 'Here's a choice of 25 experiences you can have, first-come, first-served. We will try to match you up with your first choice'", Wayne Johnson, the retired senior vice president and chief human resources officer of Maple Leaf Foods, told me. "It could be a budget meeting, it could be a customer meeting, or it could be at a systems review".

Other experiences for the board members include a day in the life of a sales executive, organizing fresh pork shipments across the border, or shadowing one business's management team as part of the annual budget process.

Said Johnson: "The board members might not know the people all that well, but they do know what part of the company they want to dig into. It works really well. It's a big hit."

What makes Board Connect so clever, in my view, is the way in which something so simple has such a big impact on the board. Directors get to be observers for a day. They're in the field, spending time with the leaders and future leaders of the company. It's an opportunity for them to understand these individuals better and to see how these high performers behave. Through this, they get a better understanding of the culture—the directors get to feel the culture and to see how day-to-day decisions are made.

More organizations should have programs like this. If they don't, they should be looking at ways in which the board can support and help set the cultural direction of the company, or they should be supporting the CEO in those efforts.

Also, consider this: if your board doesn't have a real understanding of your culture, how can it help the organization during a major transition?

A case in point here is Tim Hortons. In May 2011, it was announced that Don Schroeder, the president and CEO of Tim Hortons since 2008—who had been with the organization in different capacities for 20 years—would no longer be serving in his current role.[3] Executive chairman Paul House assumed the interim position, and the board commenced the search for a new CEO.

In this country, Tim Hortons is known as much for its culture as it is for its coffee. The board's understanding of this culture is critical, especially now.

"I think we've done a reasonably good job of educating the board about our culture. They're very supportive, and they've come in with a pretty good knowledge of our culture and a great respect for it", Paul House told me recently as I sat down for an interview with House and with the senior vice president of human resources, Brigid Pelino. "With the changes we are going through right now, the culture is the most important thing. We pick the next CEO sometime in the next few months, and we don't want somebody coming in here to change the culture".

"In any new hire, culture is what causes them typically to fail", added Pelino. "It's easy to figure out skill, but whether or not they fit is where it falls down, and that cannot be more important than at the CEO level. The number one thing the board will be recruiting for and looking at is culture. It's easy to find people who can run a business of this size. But there are very few who could run it and maintain the Tim Hortons culture".

Darren Entwistle, the president and CEO of TELUS, a leading national telecommunications company in Canada that we'll learn more about in the next chapter, also notes the important role that the board can play. In his view, without a solid understanding of the organization's culture, the board can't fulfill its role adequately.

"What's most telling is that the board has supported the culture of TELUS when it was decidedly inconvenient", Entwistle told me over the phone from Vancouver. Entwistle was referring to the recent recession, which TELUS saw as an opportunity to grow and to invest. The board supported that viewpoint.

"That took courage, and all of the governance that sanctioned that came from the board. The signal that sends to management is that they have sufficient confidence in the strategy, the people, and the leadership of the organization, and in our balance sheet, to do the opposite of what every one of our peers were pursuing at that juncture."

There are several ways to engage your board to support culture effectively.

How to Get Your Board Engaged In Culture

- Find board members who see culture as a priority and make them mentors.
- Talk about culture in board orientation programs.
- Give board members access to your organization to learn more about your culture.
- Allow board members to challenge the existing culture and to suggest ways for improving it.

1. Find Board Members Who See Culture as a Priority and Make Them Mentors

First, and as noted previously, seek out directors who value culture to become a part of your board. Look for individuals who not only have an understanding of culture but, more important, view culture as an asset. Ideally, your board members should have experience working with or for other organizations where culture has been a high priority and has been seen as a key driver of performance. That kind of experience will prove invaluable for you and for your organization's senior leadership.

It's critical to find the right mix of people for the board, people who understand corporate culture and have used it effectively to support and work with CEOs. Also consider mentorship and finding a mentor for your board who truly understands culture, who can act as a guide and a resource for the CEO and for the culture she's trying to create—someone who can discuss and measure culture at the board level.

2. Talk about Culture in Board Orientation Programs

Second, provide opportunities for your board to learn more about the importance of culture as an asset. In particular, make this type of learning a part of any board orientation program. Talk about culture, and how it's a driver of performance, so that your board members gain a better understanding of it and can advise and support the CEO accordingly.

Coastal Contacts, as we said earlier, is one of the largest online retailers of contact lenses and eyeglasses in the world. Known for its strong company culture (it was recognized as the Best Emerging Organization in our Canada's 10 Most Admired Corporate Cultures of 2010 program), Coastal is also innovative because it seems to have figured out ahead of the others the important role that the board plays with respect to culture. The board and the company need to be on the same page, and Coastal takes important opportunities—like board meetings—to help the board learn as much about the culture as it can.

"Our board needed to understand that we think our core values and the type of people we're trying to attract and retain has to not just align in the company, it has to be aligned in the board, and if the board doesn't see themselves in that way, there'll be a mismatch", Coastal's CEO, Roger Hardy, told me.

Hardy says that both the organization and the board learned a lot through that process.

"When we reviewed our core values and said that this is who we are, the board said, 'Okay, so now tell us who we aren't so we can make sure that if there are characteristics of our board you're seeing as a mismatch culturally, we can make sure that we at least recognize that there's a certain way we want to communicate and operate'", recalled Hardy. "I think there are some good learnings in that. It's no good if the company is one way and the board is operating on a different level. You have to have alignment all the way through the organization".

3. Give Board Members Access to Your Organization

Third, provide your board members with access to your organization. Find ways, like Maple Leaf Foods' Board Connect, for your board members to observe how high performers in your organization act, so that they can have a better understanding of what behaviours drive performance (and therefore the culture). Board members need to have access to people in the field so that they can use the cultural knowledge they've gained to help support the CEO and set the direction for the organization.

Darren Entwistle of TELUS certainly agrees with this viewpoint, and he takes it further by arguing that sometimes the CEO needs to get out of the way.

"The board has explicitly been told, 'You don't need to go through me to talk to any of the senior leadership team'", Entwistle added. "I'm not a funnel. If you've got an issue, you've got an idea, you've got a comment, you've got a question—knock yourself out. There is no monopoly on the right way forward, and the more connected the communications are within the organization, the better, from my perspective, and I don't want to do anything that frustrates that".

4. Allow Board Members to Challenge the Existing Culture and to Suggest Ways for Improving It

Finally, allow your board members to challenge and question your existing culture. Allow them to gain a full understanding of the systems and support structures that are being used to support and measure your culture, and to keep it strong and healthy. If any of those systems are in need of overhaul, or of any kind of adjustment, be open to suggestions in those areas from your board. Board members should be aware of those initiatives that both counter and support your culture.

Conclusion

The reality is that culture is not on the radar screen of most boards. But it should be. In my view, culture is a significant asset, and it needs to be well understood across all areas of the organization—including the board. Board members need to understand what the CEO is doing to support and evolve the culture. They need to understand how the organization's systems are supporting the culture, and they need to be connected to the business in order to evaluate it. Only then can they truly help the CEO set the direction for the organization.

Chapter 15

Taking It to the Streets:
Corporate Culture
as Your Brand

A culture is made—or destroyed—by its articulate voices.

—Ayn Rand

At our Canada's 10 Most Admired Corporate Cultures gala in February of 2010, each of our 500 attendees took home a TELUS critter (in this particular case, it was a six-inch stuffed-animal version of the TELUS tree frog). For everyone in the audience, seeing a bright green tree frog at each place setting was an immediate indication that TELUS was somehow involved in our event (and it was involved, of course, as TELUS was one of our Canada's 10 winners from 2009 and was being celebrated that evening).

If you know anything about TELUS, you'll know that it is a leading national telecommunications company in Canada (with $9.9 billion in annual revenue, 12.3 million customers, and 35,000 employees), and that it provides a range of communications products and services, including data, IP, voice, entertainment, and video.[1] (It has also delivered the highest total shareholder return amongst incumbent telecommunications companies worldwide over the past 11 years – more than doubling shareholder value in the period during which CEO Darren Entwistle has been at the helm.[2])

But TELUS is also well known for its brand, as demonstrated by its tagline (or brand promise), "The Future Is Friendly." Whimsical creatures from nature, ranging from tree frogs to pot-bellied pigs, lizards, rabbits, ducks, and fish, are the images and essence of TELUS's marketing and advertising campaigns. (Really, you'd have to have your head in the sand to not be familiar with these critters and their presence in the Canadian media space.)

At our gala that night, each tree frog had a branded tag attached to it, with a dollar amount indicated. Each amount was different, and the total represented TELUS's intended donation to six Toronto-based charities (as our event was held in Toronto) that reflected the organization's focus on youth in arts and culture, health, the environment, education, and sport. Our guests could then walk out to the lobby, where six different gift boxes were situated, and place their tag into the box representing the charity they wished TELUS to make a donation to. The end result was a collective $25,000 donation from TELUS to those organizations on behalf of our gala guests.

If this weren't enough, in honour of TELUS's launch of its new 3G+ network at that time, five of our guests also got to take home a new TELUS phone—the lucky winners again identified through the critter tag.

I thought TELUS's strategy that night was brilliant because it demonstrated two things: one, it reinforced TELUS's commitment to "We Give Where We Live" (as we read in Chapter 3, TELUS was named the Most Outstanding Philanthropic Corporation globally for 2010 by the Association of Fundraising Professionals); and, two, it tied its brand promise, "The Future Is Friendly," to its culture.

High-performance organizations, like TELUS, know that brand and culture should be one and the same.

Getting Your Message Out

I call this chapter "Taking It to the Streets" to refer to the 1976 Doobie Brothers hit. This song, to me, is all about getting your message out there. In my view, organizations need to do a better job at this, specifically with reference to their culture—and in that process, they need to realize that their culture should in fact be their brand.

Bill Tayloi, the author and *Fast Company* founder, wrote about this idea in June in a column for the *Harvard Business Review Blog Network*. Based on what he's learned from organizations that are winning big despite tough economic times, Taylor said, "You can't be special, distinctive, compelling in the marketplace unless you create something special, distinctive, compelling in the workplace".[3]

In other words, your culture is your brand, and your brand is your culture.

Ask yourself these questions: how does your brand really shape your culture, and how does your culture bring your brand to life? Our view is that your culture is your brand, and your brand is your culture. Taking this approach will help your organization stand out from the crowd in a hypercompetitive marketplace. In the process, it will also connect your employees to your customers, clients, shareholders, or other external stakeholders. Your culture and your brand should be united.

Linking Brand and Culture at TELUS

When I spoke to Darren Entwistle, the president and CEO of TELUS, over the phone from Vancouver, I assumed that he would have a lot to say on this subject. And boy, was I right. In fact, I would argue that not only is Entwistle a thought leader with respect to the fine art of making your culture your brand, he's a trailblazer.

First, a quick overview of what's become of TELUS under Entwistle's leadership.

Since Entwistle became president and CEO of TELUS in 2000, the organization's brand has grown in value from a few hundred million dollars to more than $2 billion, and has been recognized as the number one brand in Canada. Here's another remarkable fact: TELUS's total shareholder returns have outperformed those of all of its global peers over the past five, six, seven, eight, nine, and ten plus years since 2000—the best results among global incumbent telecom companies. It has generated an incredible 135 percent return for shareholders since 2000.[4]

"The gap between us and our peers is monumental, and that to me is a testament to the people of the TELUS organization", Entwistle told me. "Products come and go, technology comes and goes, but what's constant is the culture being the most strategic asset of the organization. It's an achievement that belongs to the people of the TELUS organization, and we're really proud of that".

Key to all of this, in Entwistle's view, was the strategy of tying the TELUS brand—The Future Is Friendly—to the organization's four values, which are

1. We embrace change and initiate opportunity.
2. We have a passion for growth.
3. We believe in spirited teamwork.
4. We have the courage to innovate.

Said Entwistle: "We realized that the only way we were going to have integrity and live up to our brand promise with our external stakeholders—which would be clients through to investors and the public sector—would be if the brand would equally resonate as strongly internally in the hearts and minds of our employees. The model to drive that home was the value sets."

The effect of this approach, said Entwistle, was an alignment of interests.

"Adding employees to the stakeholder group is the brand resonating outward and inward", he said. "Employees are joining the clients and the investor stakeholder group. It's a friendly future brought to you by a passion for growth. It's a friendly future realized by the courage to innovate. A friendly future realized through spirited teamwork. Doing that—explicitly connecting the brand promise with the value set of the organization—was monstrous".

To further strengthen the link between the brand and the culture, Entwistle enlisted the significant heft of TELUS's marketing department, effectively turning it inward.

"We thought if TELUS as an organization has a Ph.D. in external marketing, the way we animate our brand externally through TV commercials, print, media, social networking, and the like, why don't we turn that inwards and market to ourselves and to our employees who are already so positively disposed to the brand?" said Entwistle. "And so we said, we've got such a well-developed marketing muscle, from a physical

and intellectual perspective, let's use it within the internal TELUS organization to drive a greater level of engagement, emotional connection, and
commercial affinity between our employees, our brand, our brand promise, and the values that underpin that brand promise".

Entwistle also ensured that marketing the brand internally resonated
across functions.

"This is not something that is the restricted domain of the marketing department or HR. It's something that's got to be meaningful to
Regulatory, to Legal, to Finance, and so on and so forth", said Entwistle.

Control Your Culture or It Will Control You

In 2010's *The Why of Work: How Great Leaders Build Abundant
Organizations*, authors Dave and Wendy Ulrich argue that leaders can create better, stronger organizations when they help employees clarify their own
personal identity within that organization.[5] In other words, when employees are able to find meaning in what they do at work, they contribute value
(and therefore, helping employees find that meaning is good for business).
As an executive search professional, I see that need—not just for meaning,
but also for clarity—coming from many of our candidates (especially those
from Generation Y and, to a certain extent, Generation X). Candidates are
looking for far more than a job that allows them to simply say, "I work for
the 'corp'". What they want is more along the lines of, "I associate with the
organization because . . ." Really, they want an employee life that is worth
living; they want transparency; and they want to find ways to link their own
values, beliefs, motivations, and interests with those of the organization.

If, as a leader, you are able to put your finger on what makes your
organization unique, and if you can articulate this and give it a broader
meaning for employees, it's magical: that articulation of your culture, in
effect, becomes your brand. From there, your culture already has reso-
nance with your employees, and to some degree with some external stakeholders. It can easily become the brand if you find the right
communication vehicles with which to unleash it. The message is this:
employees—and not just external groups and markets—need to be a part
of the stakeholder group for your brand.

To put it bluntly, either you control your culture or your culture will control you. If you align your employees with your culture, as we've said before, it will drive great engagement and exceptional results—with TELUS clearly being the case in point.

Another great example is WestJet and what I'll refer to as the "Owners Care" brand. The idea of WestJetters caring about what they do because they are owners was initially introduced to consumers in 2005 as a television, radio, and print campaign. The ads were really well done, quirky, and fun; they featured scenarios ranging from flight attendants chasing after customers with forgotten cell phones or helping a businesswoman who had forgotten important documents. The ads ended with the question: "Why do WestJetters care so much? Because we're also WestJet owners."

What's particularly interesting about this campaign is that it wasn't the one the airline had originally planned to go with. In fact, when it was presented to the employees at a town hall meeting, the first campaign was not met with enthusiasm at all. Called "WestJettitude", it featured light-hearted pokes and other dos and don'ts for loving WestJet. But something about the ads hit a nerve. Employees felt that the ads made fun of their roles. The campaign was so disliked that the employees complained to the airline's executive. The media for the entire campaign—television and print—had already been purchased, and the campaign was scheduled to launch in days. But the reaction from the front line was so strong that WestJet went back to the agency and asked it to pull the campaign.

"What came out of that was the passion the employees have for the organization," Duncan Bureau, the vice president of sales for WestJet, told us. "The Owners Care campaign really came out of that entire experience because WestJetters were absolutely passionate about the message that was going into the marketplace about them and about their contributions to the organization. I think the experience took the branding of the organization to an entirely new level."

Even though the airline had been in business since 1996, it was only at this point that the "we care because we're owners" mantra became the airline's brand—and it was such a perfect and obvious articulation of the company's culture. Why? Because of WestJet's Employee Share Purchase Plan and its profit-sharing program, WestJetters are owners, and they are able to articulate the idea that they care in every interaction with customers and with each other. The Owners Care mantra has become who they are, and what's so interesting about this story is that WestJetters themselves set the course for this branding. They were so clear about what they didn't like in the first campaign because they already knew what they were—and what they weren't.

For organizations that are looking for the right way to make their brand their culture and their culture their brand, here are a few things to keep in mind.

First, we've talked about the Know Thyself principle. In the process of finding your brand, ensure that you are clear on your organization's core values and behaviours. Do additional work in this area through surveys, communiqués, and focus groups with your customers, your employees, and your suppliers.

Second, find and develop the key tagline or mantra that articulates who you are and resonates with both your internal and external stakeholder groups.

Third, hire for fit. As we'll learn more about in Chapter 16, ensure that you are recruiting the right people, who live those behaviours and who can articulate who you are as an organization. Jettison those who don't. You have to be vigilant about this—not to be flippant, but to the best of your abilities, make sure that everyone is drinking the Kool-Aid.

Also, as we talked about in other chapters, ensure that you're training for those behaviours. In addition, you really have to understand how you further support those behaviours—for instance, through reward and recognition, as we've discussed.

And finally, as you would expect, the leaders in the organization have to communicate the brand and the culture. Again, WestJet does this really well with its quarterly Culture Connection sessions, where executives and WestJetters get together to talk about their culture.

This is a critical point: for culture to become brand and brand to become culture, it has to be clearly articulated. Don't just rely on your HR department to do so, or let HR and Marketing work on this messaging independent of each other. Some of the best companies we've worked with understand that articulating brand as culture should be a joint partnership between Marketing and Human Resources.

For instance, as many as eight years ago, RBC, Canada's largest bank and one of North America's leading diversified financial services companies, had already aligned these two functions under Elisabetta Bigsby (now retired). Bigsby was the global head of human resources and transformation for RBC.[6] This was the first time I'd seen Marketing and HR under one umbrella, and I thought it was an incredibly innovative tactic for aligning culture within an organization—not to mention being ahead of its time.

The point I'm making is that you really need to zero in on who you are as an organization in order to develop your brand. This isn't about finding a unique positioning in the marketplace. Why? Because that positioning probably has nothing to do with your culture. These days, your brand is going to be defined by your employees and by your customer experiences—whether you're a business-to-business or business-to-consumer business. It's all out there online, so ensure that you're in control of it as much as possible, and if it's going to be out there regardless, make sure that you've got your brand figured out and clearly articulated.

It's really about closing the loop, if you will: if you make your culture the brand and the brand your culture, you'll be better positioned for stronger performance. No longer can organizations channel communications based on audience segments. The audience is now "one" because of the speed of the Internet and of communications in general. It's best to structure your brand so that it resonates with employees and to ensure that you are who you say you are. It's time for all hands on deck—marketing, HR, GMs, and others—to find out who you are and to align your entire communications and brand around it.

Chapter 16

Recruiting for Fit

Every man's ability may be
strengthened or increased by culture.

—John Abbott

A NUMBER OF YEARS AGO, I asked a client if he could describe his company's culture—if he could tell us what it was that the company was all about. Without hesitating, he said, "Yes, I can: we're quirky, we're edgy, and we're cynical".

Obviously, that was a very blunt—not to mention refreshingly honest—answer to a very important question, especially for us as the search partner. And in the case of this client, it was an absolutely accurate description of the type of candidate that succeeded within his organization. This company was enormously successful at finding the right people precisely because they knew what they were looking for—the "quirky-edgy-cynical" candidate, as strange as it may sound, was the perfect cultural fit for this organization. People with these behaviours were its high performers.

In our 2011 Canadian Corporate Culture Study, 85 percent of respondents indicated that cultural fit is more important than necessary skills when hiring.[1] That's a stunning number, although in our world, it's not surprising. We noticed early on in our executive search practice that clients were placing more importance on fit—as in defined behaviours—when hiring. Furthermore, the successful candidate placements (the longer tenures) were far more common when the client focused on finding the right cultural fit, rather than relying solely on an exact skill set. In other words, when organizations focused on hiring people based on how they thought a person would fit with their culture and how that person's behaviour was similar to the behaviours of the company's existing high performers, it tended to be a more successful hire in the long term.

Look up a definition for corporate culture and you'll usually come across wording that defines it as a combination of the beliefs and values of an organization. But as we've discussed, culture is really about collective behaviour—that is, the collective behaviour of the organization.

For many organizations, defining their culture is a bit of a hurdle. In our business, we're amazed at how many times in the course of a year we're asked to help an organization understand and define its culture. It's incredible. The reality is that all organizations have a culture. Knowing that culture is critically important in recruiting for fit.

So how do you hire for fit? After years of experience working with high-performance candidates in our executive search practice, and after having gone through thousands of interviews and submissions for our Canada's 10 Most Admired Corporate Cultures program, here are a few things to consider.

Best Practices in Recruiting for Fit

1. Find Your Key Success Behaviours— Know Thyself and Know Others

Finding successful people isn't enough anymore—it's finding out *how* they're successful that's really important.

Ask yourself this question: how do the most successful people in your organization behave? The best way to start the process of answering this question is to construct a culture index: look at the most successful people in your organization, and identify five or six common behaviours that they share. In other words, spend some time with your high performers and find behavioural themes that are consistent among those

Best Practices in Recruiting for Fit

- Find your key success behaviours—know thyself and know others
- Practice continuous/active recruitment—make recruitment an "all-the-time" activity
- Screen and interview for fit—"ABC" it (always behavioural and chronological)
- Get beyond the interview
- Seek the opinions of others
- Conduct directed referencing
- Integrate

high performers. The reality is that the people who are currently successful in your organization are the key to finding the right kind of new talent. We see this time and time again in our search work.

But don't stop at what your high performers have accomplished within your own organization. Look at the types of cultures in which those individuals generated their past results. Furthermore, keep a list of organizations that have cultures similar to yours. As we'll see in the next step, both of these processes are critical to arming yourself with a virtual bench of talent that will be available when—not if—you need it.

2. Practice Continuous/Active Recruitment— Make Recruitment an "All-the-Time" Activity

Great organizations practice active recruitment. This means that they look a few years down the road and build a virtual bench of people whom they may or may not need to recruit. This is critically important if your organization has high rates of churn or other shorter-term succession needs. Practicing active recruitment requires a lot of heavy lifting, but it's a time- and cost-effective approach, and the process can provide organizations with a critical short list of candidates when needed.

The reality is that most organizations wait until the point when they need to start hiring before they start recruiting. We're constantly amazed by this. But taking the time to research and source the kind of talent your organization will need in the future—that is, the virtual bench—is a difficult task. It's not something that every organization is equipped to do.

Obviously, recruiting firms can help with this by targeting specific industries and organizations within those industries, and finding the individuals who have the right titles who might fit a specific role.

Aside from bringing a search partner on board, organizations need to enlist their HR practitioners to practice (and teach) active and continuous recruitment. Challenge those individuals, on a daily basis, to be researching and developing your organization's virtual bench.

Ideally, a virtual bench ensures that for the top two or three positions in your management or leadership team, you have at least two or three potential candidates in the wings. Those candidates may not currently be in your organization. They might also be passive—that is, not looking for new opportunities—rather than active. But knowing who these individuals are gives your organization a significant competitive advantage in terms of your ability to recruit for fit.

Developing a virtual bench will also make your organization better at recruitment, because you'll be constantly going out into the market. You will have active and benchmarked candidates who can be used in your recruitment efforts.

3. Screen and Interview for Fit—"ABC" It (Always Behavioural and Chronological)

Technical and skill competencies are a price of entry for any candidate these days. Behaviour—that is, how the person does things, as measured against the cultural index of the existing successful people within your organization—needs to be front and centre.

The first place to start in this process is with the chronological interview.

Not everyone believes in the chronological interview. I see professionals in my own field start with the candidate's current-day roles and move backwards through her career. But if you want to understand not just the professional but the person behind the role, to learn about how a candidate was and is successful, to find out how she thinks, to find trends in her behaviour, and so on, the chronological interview is a critical step in that process.

Here are the basic steps in performing a chronological interview:

- Ask questions starting with a candidate's education and moving forward. This allows you to examine how the candidate's life has unfolded.
- Story is everything; ask for the story of the candidate's career, and you will get the story of his life as his career has unfolded.
- Look for career transitions—those stops along the road when a candidate moved from one position to another or from one organization to the next—and ensure that you understand why those transitions took place. What was going on in the candidate's mind when she made that particular change from one position to the next? How did she end up where she ended up? Was she recruited? Who were the key influencers in the decision—was it family or friends? What are the trends? Why a candidate made a particular move at a particular time tells you how she thinks.
- Collect names along the way and find out whom the candidate reported to at each stage.
- Find the links between how a candidate thinks and what he's done, and look for trends in those behaviours (history repeats itself; candidates with a successful track record are far more likely to keep on being successful).
- Examine the types of environments the candidate worked in, and find out why they worked and why they didn't. Did the candidate perform better in larger organizations or in smaller, more entrepreneurial places? Also, ask the candidate how she viewed the cultural environment of her previous workplaces, and why it did (or didn't) make her successful.
- Look for gaps that will require further examination. The face-to-face interview is just the starting point in the hiring-for-fit process. It's always preceded by a phone assessment, which the candidate has presumably passed. In our firm, our researchers are highly skilled at this. From assessment to sell or from assessment to punt, the first

call with a candidate pulls critical initial data on whether the candidate potentially has the right background and/or is the right fit for the role. Even if the candidate progresses to the face-to-face interview and passes, the interviewer's job is to perform further research into any gaps that may have appeared during the process.

4. Get Beyond the Interview

The chronological interview serves as a "gut check" on what's real and whether or not what the person is saying makes sense. In addition to the initial phone assessment, it's the data collection vehicle. The interview is a conversation in which you get the facts and find out what doesn't add up. From there, it's important that you move into real discussions about the person to see both how he works and how he thinks. It's kind of like a first date, when both parties keep things safe by meeting for coffee—and from there, you can determine if there's enough to take it to the next level.

To get beyond the interview, the next step is to determine the candidate's behavioural style and to find ways to discover who she is as a person. Understanding the person—not just the professional—is critical in recruiting for fit. But it's not an easy task, especially if the candidate is well honed and knows how to answer each question the right way. There are also some stickier considerations when you're trying to find out all you can about a candidate. Clients are often concerned about how much they can ask, depending on various laws in their jurisdiction, for instance. The key here is to seek as much information as you can by asking open-ended questions, such as, "What do you do in your spare time? What are your passions and interests outside of work?"

Here are a few tips for getting beyond the interview:

- Create a comfortable setting. When people are comfortable and you have created a warm setting for them, they tend to speak more freely.
- Give them time to settle. Let a candidate sit for three to five minutes between one interaction and the next, so that he can get used to the environment he's in.
- Find out about a candidate's interests, passions, and beliefs.
- Find out what the candidate likes to do outside of work.

- Conduct additional and multiple noninterview meetings. Move the candidate into additional discussions (such as 100-day plans, business case discussions, SWOT analysis, and so on). These serve as great measurements of actual behaviour, and you can observe how the person works. Other ideas include lunches, dinners, or meetings with the candidate and her spouse. One client of ours likes to meet his potential candidates on the ski hill on a Saturday afternoon, in ski gear and snow boots, just to see the person in a different environment. In fact, in one particular case, this client was considering going with someone else until he spent a few hours on the hill with the alternative candidate (who eventually landed the role).

Another client came to me a number of years ago and said that he wanted to measure the resourcefulness of the final candidate. This was not a public company with huge resources; it was a privately held organization, and it wanted to see what the candidate could do with very little. On our recommendation, the candidate was given the task of putting together a 100-day plan to see where he would go with it.

This candidate—who ultimately was offered the position—did an incredible job on the 100-day plan, talking to customers, talking to suppliers, and going out into the field. He was given virtually no data, and what he showed was incredible resourcefulness. It was enormously impressive behaviour, and, more important, it was the kind of behaviour the client was looking for. The candidate was one of the best we've ever placed.

5. Seek the Opinions of Others

Relying on two or three individuals on a search committee to interview and hire a candidate is an all-too-common approach—well intentioned, but misguided, especially if you're looking to hire for fit.

In fact, including others in the decision-making process is critical.

There's no rule as to how many others you should include in the process, and there's a bit of a law of diminishing returns effect: it's more than three, and probably less than six or seven. How's that for accurate? The key is to incorporate the opinions of others—more important, others with different styles.

Here are a few guidelines when you are seeking the opinions of others:

- *Involve your judgment stars.* Who are the individuals within your organization who have great judgment, who will tell you what you may not want to hear? Judgment stars are trained cynics, individuals who tend to look at things in a different way from the way you or your client would. Give these individuals the opportunity to meet the candidate and to spend time with her. Because of their worldview, judgment stars are invaluable when recruiting for fit (they can also be of great help in integrating the candidate).
- *Debrief together.* When you are incorporating the opinions of others, remember to debrief together. At a minimum, put the search professional, the HR leader, and the hiring manager together on a conference call, and ensure that someone is capturing the information. Failing to do so means that you miss the opportunity to listen to the observations of others—to hear about the same things you observed.
- *Use individuals you wouldn't normally use.* We have a great benefit in our firm in that candidates come to us—our office—for interviews. And because of that, the candidate is probably going to meet about four different people in our firm in the process: the researcher who had the initial contact with the candidate, the client services individual who booked the meeting, the person at reception, and the partner (or whoever is doing the interview).

Think about that—think about how valuable this feedback is in the hiring process. How did the candidate treat the person at reception? What was your frontline person's impression? This kind of feedback is invaluable, but is often missed. The tendency is to cycle the candidate through the process quickly. But you're missing a golden opportunity if you don't talk with your other team members and share information.

The old adage "hire slow and fire fast" is true. More to the point, don't be afraid to deal with something if it comes up. If your candidate was a bit of a jerk to the receptionist when you were out of earshot, then maybe you have a problem. If someone has a concern, discuss it, flush it out, and talk about it.

6. Conduct Directed Referencing

When I first started in the search business in the early 2000s, there was one thing that really concerned me about how candidates were recruited, and that was the process of checking references. To me, it always seemed broken. Think about it: we ask candidates to submit the names of individuals who will act as references on their behalf. What do we think we're going to get in return? Nothing but "wonderful" (and if we're not getting at least that, we have other problems).

As a starting point, we should be asking for the names of the people the candidate has reported to and the names of professional colleagues or other individuals who have reported to the candidate. It also dawned on me early in the business and in talking to other professionals that to truly make referencing relevant, we should be looking at all of the names that we collect during the interview process. What else? We should focus on the network of people that we, as the search partner, might also know. Social networking is a great tool for this, as it increases our likelihood of having a connection with the candidate.

The point that it's important to take away here is that we should be directing the process and providing the candidate with a list of names of people that we want to speak to, in conducting the referencing process, as opposed to the candidate's supplying us with the list. Directed referencing takes out the bias and creates a whole different type of discussion.

Ask yourself this question: what kind of information do you want to get from a reference? If it's all champagne and roses, that's not always a good thing. You're not looking for negative information, but what you do want is the full picture of the candidate—who the person is and how his behaviour in the past might align with what makes for success within your own organization.

Clearly the main challenge with directed referencing is that you can't compromise a candidate's current employment. This is a clear instance of how a search partner with other trusted relationships is better poised to get the information. But don't expect a perfect report on the candidate—and that's not a bad thing. Directed referencing not only arms an employer with information for a hiring decision, but also provides the kind of intelligence that can do double duty as a development tool should the candidate be hired.

7. Integrate

Integrating a new candidate into your organization and into its culture is critical. Unfortunately, it's also the stage where the ball is most commonly dropped.

Integrating your candidate goes beyond showing her where her office is and explaining the benefits package. It's about managing the candidate's expectations as she starts her job and also managing the expectations of the person who hired her.

Let's look at some data first.

In our 2011 Canadian Corporate Culture Study, just under 20 percent of respondents said that they did not have a process for integrating new leaders into their organizations[2] (that figure is down from about 60 percent from six years ago, so that's good news at least).

Of those who did have a process for integrating new talent, about 30 percent worry about those candidates only for the first 90 days. And about 40 percent leave the integration process to the new hire's direct report.[3]

There are some big mistakes here.

Integration should be about using what you know about the candidate's behaviour. It's about measuring the behaviours early on to see whether you got what you thought you got and to allow you to make course corrections early if necessary.

Let's use the example of a 100-day plan, developed with the candidate in conversation with the client. It can be a great integration tool.

The typical expressive right-brain communicator will take her 100-day plan and run with it like she's running for prime minister. She'll meet with everyone. She'll develop a good system to create clear, focused deliverables. On the other hand, the more left-brained, analytical candidate is going to start knocking off tasks right away and forget whom he's supposed to be communicating with. In short, he's going to need some help.

To deal with those behaviours in the integration phase, the HR team and/or the search partner need to have a good discussion with the candidate at the 30-day mark and again at the 60-day mark. These time frames act as your early detection system if problems are arising. Maybe the candidate feels that he's not getting enough time from his boss. He recognizes that he was hired because the company wanted someone who is independent and doesn't require a lot of hand-holding, but perhaps the candidate still feels that he needs a bit more access to the person he reports to.

When you are integrating a new hire, look for the behaviours that you saw in the recruitment phase and encourage those behaviours if you're not seeing them. The HR team and the search partner should be doing this, not the direct report. It's too difficult for that person to manage, and you won't get the kind of communication you need.

Facilitation from a third party—like a search partner—can also be of great assistance when assessing the early integration of a candidate.

Chapter 17

Performance
Management for Fit

The only thing of real importance that leaders
do is to create and manage culture. If you do not manage
culture, it manages you, and you may not even be aware
of the extent to which this is happening.

— EDGAR SCHEIN

BRIGID PELINO, the senior vice president of human resources at Tim Hortons, does a great job of summing up the link between recruiting for fit and performance management. Here's what she told me recently:

> *Recruitment is an art, not a science. You try to build that in at the front end so that you're clear on trying to bring in people who have, who espouse, your values, and then you teach it in the orientation. So you say, "This is what we stand for". You set the expectations around behaviour while you're teaching them about the company. Then you build it into performance management—it's not just what you do; it's about the commentary around how you do it. It's never perfect, but the key is you're talking about it. You're talking about the "how"—how we expect you to behave around here as a leader, as an employee, etc.*

That's the value of these types of systems. It forces some conversation that may not be there otherwise. The best leaders will have that conversation anyway.

If hiring for fit is a critical step in finding the right people for your organization, ensuring that your performance management systems are also focused on fit is equally as important. With a well-designed plan and good training, you can build a culture of performance that will improve every part of your organization.

Performance management is about behaviour; it's about finding ways, through the development of formal systems and through the alignment of goals and objectives, to recognize the "how" in your organization. The ultimate goal of performance management is to make it easier for employees, managers, and leaders in the organization to understand that their success in the company is dependent on *how* they do things, not just *what* they do. Building a strong culture of performance is critical for meeting challenges, for promoting the things that are important to your organization, and for developing top teams. It fosters a vision whereby everyone is focused on finding ways to drive the value of who you are as an organization throughout the business—to support and promote culture.

**Building a Performance Management
Culture in Your Organization**

- Develop clearly measurable goals and objectives for behaviour and results
- Look for ongoing and positive coaching opportunities
- Communicate
- Celebrate, reward and recognize
- Make it ongoing

Here's how you can implement a performance management culture in your organization.

1. Develop Clearly Measurable Goals and Objectives for Behaviour and Results

At least 50 percent of your performance appraisals should be about the "how". Why? Because your culture is about "how"—it's not just about outcomes and not just about results. If you're not measuring your behaviour as part of performance management, then start doing so. Figure out what your core behaviours are and start measuring them. Otherwise, the message you're sending to your employees is that only outcomes matter, regardless of how they're obtained.

We've talked in earlier chapters about how organizations like Maple Leaf Foods and Yellow Media are using behaviour as half the measure of an individual's performance. But another great example is TELUS.

As we saw in an earlier chapter, when president and CEO Darren Entwistle came on board with the organization in 2000, he and his team developed the organization's four values: we embrace change and initiate opportunity, we have a passion for growth, we believe in spirited teamwork, and we have the courage to innovate.

At about the same time, it was also decided that 50 percent of performance bonuses for management would be tied to those values.

"For us, it was pretty simple", Entwistle told me. "We're going to recognize you for what you get done and for how you realize those achievements in a manner that is consistent with the four values".

He added: "For the management community, being the leaders of this company, 50 percent of your in-year performance bonus is going to be tethered to what you get done against the personal performance objective that you have set yourself and agreed to with your support person. The other 50 percent in terms of your in-year performance bonus is going to be contingent on *how* you realized those accomplishments".

Like TELUS, make sure that behaviours are measurable. Many people will argue that behaviours are difficult to measure. Not necessarily. If you want your employees to be innovative, for instance, go out and find people who behave in an innovative way. From there, ensure that during the course of the year, you're finding ways to catch and record these individuals behaving in that way. That's what measuring behaviour is really all about. Come to a performance review, for instance, armed with examples that you can share with your employee—for example, "Here's where you did these things and exhibited these behaviours, and that was great". If you don't do so, the behaviours aren't really valuable. It's also helpful for people to measure themselves and record their own behaviour (which is what we do in our firm). Leaders may be the ones to outline what they want an employee to achieve, but sometimes it can also be very effective to ask the employee to think about how he's going to do it.

2. Look for Ongoing and Positive Coaching Opportunities

Leaders have to ensure that they're regularly on the lookout for opportunities to reinforce the right behaviours. Employees should never be walking into a performance review thinking: "I wonder how I did", or, "I wonder what she's going to say". That's because ideally they've been coached throughout the year. People want to be caught doing things well. Like your own children, they want positive reinforcement. Failure is an opportunity for growth, yes. But if you're giving feedback only when individuals aren't performing, you're going to create a culture of people who do not want to be observed. Coaching—and looking for positive coaching opportunities to reinforce good behaviour—is the key. That way, when performance review time rolls around, you're talking about things that have already been discussed and looking for additional opportunities to drive that employee's engagement.

3. Communicate

Talking about and celebrating behaviour are also key elements of performance management. Your recognition and rewards systems should allow you to communicate to the employee base that a certain individual has represented a core behaviour through his actions. Communicate this—loudly and proudly—because if you talk about things, you are managing people's expectations about how they act. Also, tell stories about customers and employees that represent the culture. Employees are more interested in these types of stories than they are in the ones that focus only on earnings and results or on how the organization is doing against plan.

4. Celebrate, Reward, and Recognize

Rewarding people is part of performance management, not something separate that happens after the fact. The important thing to remember is that individuals should be recognized and rewarded based on their behaviours and not just on what they accomplished, as in "I really appreciate *how* you did this".

Again, a great example of how to do this well comes from TELUS.

"We built our recognition system explicitly around our core values, but we also built our rewards in a way that would customize to the values themselves and the recognition that we wanted to engender within the team member", Entwistle told me.

So, for instance, Entwistle told me that in the case of TELUS and the four values listed earlier, this might mean that an individual might be recognized for having the "courage to innovate". That person would then be granted points and could go into the company store and purchase lifestyle prizes that were actually designed to represent innovation and courage.

"The reward is specific to the value", added Entwistle. "Or let's say we recognized individuals for their 'spirited teamwork'. We said, you know what? Let's not artificially constrain the definition of teamwork to the tele-company specifically. Why doesn't teamwork also mean their families and their communities? So the prizes could be something as simple as, 'You were fantastic; here's dinner and movie tickets for you and your entire family to go out and spend time together because you couldn't have made the contribution that you made, which came with personal sacrifice, without the support of your family'".

This is a great example of rewards being tied to values (and to the associated behaviours). It's additionally reinforced by bringing in an individual's family to share in the recognition—which I think is a very smart added touch.

5. Make It Ongoing

Generally speaking, if performance management is something that takes place once or twice a year, if it is based solely on outcomes and not at all on behaviours, and if it's not continual, it's not going to be aligned with the culture. It will also be likely to be a process that's met with resistance.

Conclusion

If you do nothing other than judge the people in your organization based on whether or not they're aligned with the core values of your organization, you'll be ahead of the pack in terms of performance management. Ideally, you want to strive to do more, but that's a good start. Performance management for fit is really about behaviour—it's about focusing on what the desired behaviours are, recognizing and rewarding them, recording the right behaviours when you see them, and finding ways to keep those behaviours alive. It should be integrated into your formal systems, like performance reviews, recognition, and rewards, and into your communication vehicles. Performance management for fit reinforces culture and optimizes results by aligning the parts of the organization. But you've got to start with measuring behaviour. If it's just about outcomes, you'll never get there.

Chapter 18

Culture and Performance: Proof Positive That Culture Is More than Connected to Performance — It Drives Performance

---

Culture eats strategy for breakfast.

— Peter Drucker

What's Been Said about Culture and Performance

TELUS

Darren Entwistle, president and CEO of TELUS (one of Canada's 10 Most Admired Corporate Cultures of 2009):

> *The reason we were so enthusiastic, from emotional to academic, in our embracing of culture is because we saw a significantly sustainable competitive advantage that we could engineer over the competition. The competition can try and copy some of our strategy, they could copy some of our HR performance techniques, they could try to emulate our marketing from a brand perspective, but what they couldn't do was replicate our culture. That was the root motivation behind the effort we put into it.[1]*

TELUS's Performance:
- TELUS's total returns have outperformed those of all of its global peers over the five, six, seven, eight, nine, and ten plus years since 2000, generating a 135 percent return for shareholders.[2]

Four Seasons Hotels and Resorts

Isadore Sharp, founder and chairman, Four Seasons Hotels and Resorts (Canada's 10 Most Admired Corporate Cultures Hall of Fame):

> *The reason for our success is no secret. It comes down to one single principle that transcends time and geography, religion and culture. It's the Golden Rule—the simple idea that if you treat people well, the way you would like to be treated, they will do the same.*[3]

Four Seasons Hotels and Resorts' Performance:
- Grown from a single hotel to 85 hotels in 35 different countries around the world over the past 50 years.[4]
- Four Seasons Hotel New York named the best-performing hotel in the luxury segment by Smith Travel Research after being evaluated on occupancy, ADR (average daily rate), and RevPAR (revenue per available room) in year-over-year comparison.[5]
- Four Seasons Resort Whistler won the AAA/CAA Five Diamond Award in 2011, making it the only Five Diamond hotel or resort in Canada.[6]

Acklands-Grainger Inc.

Court Carruthers, senior vice president, Grainger; president, international businesses in Canada (Acklands-Grainger Inc.) (one of Canada's 10 Most Admired Corporate Cultures of 2009):

> *It's not the infrastructure, it's not the inventory, it's not the strong financial backing—it's not that. It's the fact that we have this great resource base of focused team members who have a winning attitude, who know the giant has woken up, who feel con-*

fident that what they do is keep Canadian businesses running and keep Canadian employers and employees safe.[7]

Acklands-Grainger Inc.'s Performance:
- Had its best quarter in the history of the company in the first quarter of 2011, with revenue growth of 18 percent (profits improved more than 300 percent).[8]
- Made more money in the first quarter of 2011 than in all of 2006—30 percent more.[9]

Yellow Media
Marc Tellier, president and CEO of Yellow Pages Group (Canada's 10 Most Admired Corporate Cultures Hall of Fame), CEO of Canpages, and CEO of Trader Corporation:

> *Culture will drive your performance. I could use endless lame sports analogies. But if you don't have a healthy dynamic in any locker room, you're dead. You might win sometimes, but you're not going to consistently win. Culture is a precursor to success.*[10]

Yellow Media's Performance:
- Revenues increased from $613 million in 2003 to $1.4 billion in 2010, a compound annual growth rate (CAGR) of 13 percent.[11]
- EBITDA increased from $401 million in 2003 to $757 million in 2010, a CAGR of 10 percent.[12]

WestJet
Ferio Pugliese, executive vice president, people and culture, WestJet (Canada's 10 Most Admired Corporate Cultures Hall of Fame):

> *I believe at WestJet, our culture jumps off the walls at us. If I had to think about how we'll evolve, the one thing we'll need to stick true to is our fundamental principles about care and ownership, and I think through that we'll withstand any kind of challenge this business will throw at us.*[13]

WestJet's Performance:

- WestJet is one of the most profitable airlines in North America.[14]
- 2010 earnings before tax (EBT) margin of 7.5 percent was once again one of the best in the North American airline industry.[15]
- Named a J.D. Power 2011 Customer Service Champion.[16]
- Highest-ranked airline based on brand equity in an August 2010 syndicated study conducted by Harris/Decima (other airlines measured in the study were Air Canada, American Airlines, British Airways, Porter Airlines, Southwest Airlines, United Airlines, and Virgin Atlantic).[17]

Tim Hortons

Brigid Pelino, senior vice president, human resources, Tim Hortons (Canada's 10 Most Admired Corporate Cultures Hall of Fame):

> *You have the best people, with the right experience, with a passion for what they do under consistent visionary leadership. It's a winning combination.*[18]

Tim Hortons' Performance:

- Growth: From 100 employees and 200 stores in 1985 to 2,000 employees and 3,782 systemwide restaurants in 2011 (3,169 in Canada and 613 in the United States).[19]
- North American's fourth-largest publicly traded restaurant company measured by market capitalization.[20]
- Have 41 percent share of quick service restaurant traffic in Canada.[21]
- More than 40 percent of guests in Canada visit a Tim Hortons four times or more each week.[22]

Fairmont Hotels and Resorts

Carolyn Clark, senior vice president of human resources, Fairmont Hotels and Resorts (one of Canada's 10 Most Admired Corporate Cultures of 2009):

> *We realized that bricks and mortar alone do not make for successful outcomes. To be truly successful, we had to put as much*

strategic effort into creating a people culture and a service culture as we did into the hotels.[23]

Fairmont Hotels and Resorts' Performance:
- Growth: Portfolio of 56 hotels worldwide, with plans to develop more than 20 new properties in the coming years in destinations as diverse as Shanghai, Abu Dhabi, and Anguilla.[24]
- Awards: 10 of Fairmont's properties in the United States, Canada, and Kenya appeared on *Travel & Leisure*'s Top 100 list for 2011, and 12 Fairmont properties appeared on the *Condé Nast Traveler*'s Gold List, also in 2011.[25]

CN
Hunter Harrison, (retired) president and CEO, CN:

If you get the culture right, the rest of it will almost take care of itself.[26]

CN's Performance:
- In 1995, the company was privatized and sold in the largest IPO at the time in Canada for $2.25 billion. In early 2010, the market cap for CN was an incredible $30 billion.[27]
- Under Hunter Harrison's leadership, CN's operating ratio (a measurement of efficiency in the railway industry; essentially, expenses divided by revenues) went from over 100 percent (the worst railroad in North America) to 58 percent (16 points ahead of the competition).[28]

The Importance of Culture

I've included these quotes as a reminder of why culture is so important. The case is made right from the beginning of this book that culture is the single greatest asset that an organization can have. From the first chapter, we've looked at what leaders need to do to turn culture into that asset, from knowing thyself and gaining an understanding of your organization's culture as a first step, to examining the behaviours of your top performers and rewarding and reinforcing those behaviours, to implementing key tools to align culture throughout your organization. We've seen through interviews, stories, and case studies how different leading organizations have realized that culture was or could be their true competitive advantage.

Now, in this final chapter, the material and quotes given here are reminders of why great organizations see culture as something so valuable. For me, the quotes are in many ways sources of inspiration.

Why?

Because, as management consultant Peter Drucker once famously said, culture eats strategy for breakfast. To me that means: forget everything else. If you get culture right, it will drive the right behaviour, and the behaviour will drive results. Get culture wrong, and forget your strategy—disaster will strike.

I can think of no better example than Nortel. In 1999, the lion's share of the TSX 300 at the time was one company, Nortel, with $30 billion in sales and 95,000 employees. Everyone wanted Nortel stock, and even when it started to plummet there was still a thrill at the idea of getting it for a cheaper price because of the overall view that it would eventually go back up—I can remember buying stock at $28 and then getting it at $8, and then at $5. We all know what happened from there.

Nortel's problem? It was so heavily focused on the price of its stock that its culture got out of whack. Yes, there was an alleged improper use of accrued liabilities, a restating of the financials on the balance sheet, and other forms of cookie-jar accounting that I won't get into here. The point I want to make is that everything went so wrong because Nortel forgot what made it such a great organization in the first place: it was innovation. Nortel was an innovative telco, and it was on top of the world, with a leading CEO in John Roth (named CEO of the year in 2000) to boot.

But its culture became one of public reporting rather than innovation. And even if it had the most innovative organization developing the most innovative technologies in the telecom space and doing phenomenal acquisitions of the best companies, the culture became only about those acquisitions. It became about continuing to drive the top line for the sake of the public markets. In doing so, its leaders became focused on the wrong things and, as a result of that, effectively broke the law.

So you take this giant company, with an astonishing pool of innovative workers and enormous shareholder confidence and support, and you turn it into a basket case of accounting scandal, self-serving management, and stunningly complacent directors. Instead of a culture of innovation, you get a culture of arrogance and greed, where the one and only thing that Nortel felt it needed to do was to make money. This is perhaps an extreme example of how culture eats strategy for breakfast, but it shows how leaders can turn an organization's culture into something that's so bad that it sinks the company—in this case, a $30 billion enterprise.

Canada's 10 Most Admired Corporate Cultures

As we remind ourselves again of the key role that culture plays in driving performance, it's also the perfect time to examine in more detail some of the results from our firm's Canada's 10 Most Admired Corporate Cultures program, now well into its seventh year.

As we mentioned earlier in the book, Canada's 10 is in many ways our firm's R&D lab—whether it's the thousands of leadership surveys through our Canadian Corporate Culture Study, the hundreds of Canada's 10 program submissions and interviews each year, our annual Corporate Culture Summit, our regional events, or our national Canada's 10 gala, we're fortunate to be at the forefront of best practices in culture and fit. As an executive search firm, we share those practices with our clients to help them recruit for fit, perform cultural assessments, and build great organizations.

For our purposes here, I want to do the same thing. We've talked about some of these findings at different stages throughout the book. But here's an at-a-glance. I hope that sharing this information with you serves as a great way to drive home what we've been talking about all along: culture is a competitive advantage. Figuring that out is the first step toward building a high-performance organization.

Here's some proof.

Background

First, a bit of background on the Canada's 10 program. Since 2005, our firm has been recognizing some of Canada's leading organizations for having a culture that has helped them enhance performance and sustain a competitive advantage.

Each year, about 500 organizations are nominated to the program through a peer-reviewed process. The main vehicle for our nominations is our Canadian Corporate Culture Study. The study surveys the senior leadership teams from many of Canada's top organizations—hundreds of individuals who either are at the president and/or CEO level or are in charge of the human resources/talent management side of the business.

We ask these people a variety of questions about corporate culture, including how they measure it, how they align it, the impact of leadership on culture, how they recruit and retain talent, whether they hire for cultural fit over skill, and, of course, what impact culture has on the overall performance of their organizations. At the end of the survey, we ask them to nominate the Canadian organizations they most admire for having a culture that impacts performance.

Once organizations are nominated, they are invited to make a detailed submission to the program, based on five criteria: vision and leadership; cultural alignment, measurement, and sustainability; rewards, recognition, and innovative business achievement; corporate performance; and, corporate social responsibility.

After an interview of the senior executives from each submitting organization by the partners of our firm, the submissions are then sent to our program's 25-member board of governors (largely made up of CEOs and senior HR leaders from past winners of the Canada's 10 program, who are "off the books," so to speak, from competing, as the national award has a three-year license). Our board votes first on 30 regional finalists (10 from each of the three regions: West, Central, and Quebec and Atlantic Canada), and then they choose the 10 national winners. Both regional and national winners are celebrated at different events across Canada and at our national gala, which is held annually in February in Toronto. We also choose special category winners from our emerging organizations and from the broader public-sector organizations that apply.

The program has grown significantly, particularly in the past three years. For instance, we've seen a 60 percent increase in the number of organizations proceeding with a submission from 2009 to 2011. Our gala sells out annually, with 500 senior leaders from our winning organizations filling their tables at the Four Seasons Hotel Toronto to celebrate their Canada's 10 win with team members, suppliers, and customers. We were also thrilled to be able to announce an inaugural Hall of Fame for Canada's 10 in 2009, as five organizations had won our award a remarkable four times (see Figure 18-1).

But to bring it back to the "why", as in, "Why is our Canada's 10 board choosing these particular organizations?" Because of how their respective cultures have impacted their performance.

Take our winners from 2010, for instance—the list is given in Figure 18-2.

Here again is a remarkable statistic about this group: the performance of Canada's 10 Most Admired Corporate Cultures of 2010, in terms of a three-year compound annual growth rate, significantly outpaced the

Four Seasons Hotels and Resorts
RBC
Tim Hortons
WestJet
Yellow Pages Group
Source: Waterstone Human Capital.

Figure 18-1 Canada's 10 Most Admired Corporate Cultures Inaugural Hall of Fame

Aeroplan Canada Inc. (Montreal, QC)
Blinds To Go Inc. (Montreal, QC)
Canadian Western Bank (Edmonton, AB)
Desjardins Group (Lévis, QC)
Discount Car and Truck Rentals (Toronto, ON)
Flight Centre (Vancouver, BC)
HOOPP–Healthcare of Ontario Pension Plan (Toronto, ON)
Maple Leaf Foods (Toronto, ON)
Procter & Gamble Canada (Toronto, ON)
The Home Depot Canada (Toronto, ON)

Special Category National Award – Best Emerging Organization:
Coastal Contacts (Vancouver, BC)

Special Category National Award – Broader Public Sector:
The Princess Margaret Hospital Foundation (Toronto, ON)
Source: Waterstone Human Capital.

Figure 18-2 Canada's 10 Most Admired Corporate Cultures of 2010

S&P/TSX 60 by an average of nearly 600 percent, or six times.[29] Figure 18-3 shows how Canada's 10 outperformed the S&P/TSX 60 in the three years ending December 31, 2009.

> The performance of Canada's 10 Most Admired Corporate Cultures of 2010, in terms of a three-year compound annual growth rate, significantly outpaced the S&P/TSX 60 by an average of nearly 600 percent, or six times.

Year after year we compare these data. Figure 18-4 gives our group of winners from 2009.

In the case of the 2009 winners, their performance in terms of a three-year compound annual growth rate outpaced the S&P/TSX 60 by an average of 300 percent, or three times.[30] That's not as significant as our 2010 winners, but it's still remarkable, and it again proves that an outstanding corporate culture has a significant impact on performance, and that culture is an incredibly valuable asset.

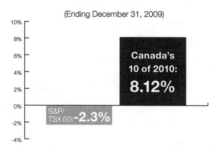

Figure 18-3   Three-Year Compound Annual Growth Rate Comparison between Canada's 10 Most Admired Corporate Cultures and the S&P/TSX 60

Acklands-Grainger Inc. (Richmond Hill, ON)
Aviva Insurance Company of Canada (Scarborough, ON)
Ceridian Canada Ltd. (Winnipeg, MB)
Corus Entertainment (Toronto, ON)
Fairmont Hotels and Resorts (Toronto, ON)
GoodLife Fitness (Toronto, ON)
Medavie Blue Cross (Moncton, NB)
Starbucks Coffee Canada (Toronto, ON)
TELUS (Vancouver, BC)
Walmart Canada (Mississauga, ON)

Source: Waterstone Human Capital.

Figure 18-4   Canada's 10 Most Admired Corporate Cultures of 2009

Our results from 2008 and earlier have showed similar outcomes. In 2008, for instance, the three-year average revenue growth and the three-year average asset growth of Canada's 10 of 2008 was 63 percent higher than those of the 60 largest public companies in Canada listed on the S&P/TSX 60.[31]

I'd like to share some other key findings from the Canadian Corporate Culture Study, each of which shows that for many of Canada's leading organizations, the relationship of culture to organizational performance is top of mind.

First, when asked whether corporate culture has an impact on performance, 85 percent of our 2011 respondents felt that it had either a strong or a very strong impact.[32]

Similarly, when we asked whether corporate culture drives performance by increasing sales and revenue, 68 percent of our respondents in 2011 felt that it did.[33]

Our findings from 2011 also reinforce the overall view our respondents have about culture being a

> *Eighty-five percent of respondents to the 2011 Canadian Corporate Culture Study felt that corporate culture had a strong or a very strong impact on corporate performance.*

strategic asset, with 56 percent seeing the alignment of culture with their organization's business strategy as an issue of importance (followed by living of values and leadership development; see Figure 18-5).[34]

		Response Percent
Alignment of culture to business strategy		55.9%
Recruitment of top talent		31.5%
Integration of new talent		14.2%
Retention of top talent		31.5%
Measurement of corporate culture		11.8%
Leadership development		43.3%
Defining of values		11.0%
Living of values		48.0%
Overall training and development		22.0%
Communication		37.8%

Source: Waterstone Human Capital, "2011 Canadian Corporate Culture Study".

Figure 18-5   What Are the Three Issues of Most Importance to You Today in Managing Your Corporate Culture?

> *Sixty-eight percent of respondents to the 2011 Canadian Corporate Culture Study believed that corporate culture drives organizational performance by increasing sales and revenue.*

These findings have told us that leading companies use cultural fit best practices so that they can recruit for fit and build great organizations.

For instance (and this finding has stayed relatively steady over the years), when asked what is more important in finding candidates for their organizations, cultural fit or necessary skills, 85 percent of our respondents in 2011 said fit (see Figure 18-6).[35]

Our study respondents felt equally strongly about the ability of their organization's culture to both acquire and retain top talent. In 2011, 85

> *Of respondents to the 2011 Canadian Corporate Culture Study, 85 percent indicated that culture impacts their ability to acquire top talent, and 86 percent said that culture impacts their ability to retain top talent.*

percent felt that culture impacted their ability to *acquire* top talent, and 86 percent felt that culture impacted their ability to *retain* top talent.[36]

In terms of how they keep their top talent retained, 82 percent of our respondents felt that keeping these individuals challenged was the best tactic, followed by advancement opportunities and training and development (see Figure 18-7).[37]

We've touched on these findings earlier in the book, but I thought revisiting them here was important. First, the percentage of our respondents measuring culture in their organizations increased from 35 percent in 2006 to 88 percent in 2011 (see Figure 18-8). In my view, this is a remarkable difference, showing clearly that over the last few years, organ-

		Response Percent
Cultural fit	████████████████████	85%
Necessary skills	████	15%

Source: Waterstone Human Capital, "2011 Canadian Corporate Culture Study".

Figure 18-6 What Is More Important in Finding Candidates for Your Organization?

		Response Percent
Higher compensation		31.0%
Better benefits		30.0%
Advancement opportunities		77.3%
Career development		74.5%
CSR policy aligned to employee goals		18.2%
Empowerment		60.0%
Keep them challenged		82.0%
Work-life balance and wellness initiatives		60.0%
Noncompete agreement		1.8%
Training and development		74.5%

Source: Waterstone Human Capital, "2011 Canadian Corporate Culture Study".

Figure 18-7 How Do You Retain Top Talent?

		Response Percent
2006		35%
2007		43%
2008		55%
2009		69%
2010		78%
2011		88%

Source: Waterstone Human Capital, "2011 Canadian Corporate Culture Study".

Figure 18-8 Percentage of Respondents Measuring Corporate Culture, 2006–2011

izations have been increasingly appreciating—in fact, placing great value on—culture within their organizations. Culture is not easy to measure, and that's one of the most difficult issues that businesspeople have with it. But you can measure behaviour, and you can build in structure that allows you to know who you are at a point in time. What's key in this finding is that it is a very important indicator that organizations are seeing culture in a strategic way.

And finally, the issue of leadership. How our respondents view leadership and its influence on the culture of an organization has also been of huge significance. In 2011, 87.5 percent of our respondents felt that leaders had the power to change corporate culture (see Figure 18-9), and 92 percent said that their current leadership has led to the evolution of their organization's corporate culture (Figure 18-10). Both points prove

	Response Percent
Yes	87.5%
No	12.5%

Source: Waterstone Human Capital, "2011 Canadian Corporate Culture Study".

Figure 18-9   Do You Believe a New Leader Can Change Your Corporate Culture?

	Response Percent
2006	38.0%
2007	37.0%
2008	81.0%
2009	88.1%
2010	90.1%
2011	92.1%

Source: Waterstone Human Capital, "2011 Canadian Corporate Culture Study".

Figure 18-10   Percentage of Respondents Indicating that Current Leadership Has Led to Evolution of Corporate Culture, 2006–2011

that leaders play a critical role in culture—with the right leader, the right tone from the top, and having someone in charge who walks and talks the culture, organizations are far better positioned to establish or maintain a winning culture.

Final Thoughts

Why is culture the greatest asset that an organization can have? It is because it's so pervasive, and it's impossible to duplicate. No two cultures are alike because culture is about behaviour, and you can't copy people's behaviours in an organization. When culture is given the focus and attention that it requires, and when it's aligned and reinforced, it is the only unique thing that an organization can truly have. Culture is the most powerful differentiator, and it's become even more powerful in today's open-source world. If you're single-minded about your culture, if you're focused, and if you create a behavioural structure that in many ways becomes self-regulating or even self-policing by your own people, culture will become your greatest advantage.

I'll close with the words of the remarkable Isadore Sharp, the founder and chairman of Four Seasons Hotels and Resorts, who writes in his book, *Four Seasons: The Story of a Business Philosophy*:

> *Over the years we've initiated many new ideas that have been copied and are now the norm in the industry. But one idea that our customers value the most cannot be copied: the consistent quality of our exceptional service. That service is based on a corporate culture, and a culture cannot be mandated as a policy. It must grow from within, based on the actions of the company's people over a long period of time.*[38]

In some ways, Sharp was the inspiration for this book. I had the good fortune to meet with him three or four years ago, and I told him about the kind of work our firm was doing on culture, and about the Canada's 10 program, in addition to our executive search. He strongly encouraged me to write this book, and now seems an appropriate time to sincerely thank him for that.

If you focus on culture, the rest takes care of itself. It seems simplistic, but this is my final piece of advice. It's a challenging and sometimes difficult journey, but if you start with culture, you'll be one step ahead of your competition in your drive to be a high-performance organization.

Canada's 10 Most Admired Corporate Cultures, 2005–2010

- Acklands-Grainger Inc. (2009)
- Aeroplan Canada Inc.(2010)
- Aviva Insurance Company of Canada (2009)
- Blinds To Go Inc.(2010)
- Boston Pizza International Inc. (2007, 2008)
- Canadian Tire Corporation (2005, 2006)
- Canadian Western Bank (2010)
- Ceridian Canada Ltd.(2009)
- Coastal Contacts Inc. (Best Emerging Organization, 2010)

- Corus Entertainment (2009)
- Dell Canada Inc (2005, 2006)
- Desjardins Group (2010)
- Discount Car and Truck Rentals (2010)
- Enbridge Inc. (Energy and Natural Resources, 2009)
- Fairmont Hotels and Resorts (2009)
- Flight Centre (2010)
- Four Seasons Hotels and Resorts (2005, 2006, 2007, 2008)
- GoodLife Fitness (2009)
- HOOPP – Healthcare of Ontario Pension Plan (2010)
- Intuit Canada (2008)
- Manulife Financial (2006, 2007)
- Maple Leaf Foods Inc (2007, 2010)
- Medavie Blue Cross (2009)
- McDonald's Restaurants of Canada Ltd. (2008)
- Microsoft Canada Co. (2006)
- Mount Sinai Hospital (Public Sector, 2009)
- Purolator Courier Ltd. (2007, 2008)
- Procter & Gamble Canada (2010)
- RBC (2005, 2006, 2007, 2008)
- Research in Motion Ltd. (2006)
- Rothmans Inc. (2005)
- Shoppers Drug Mart (2008)
- Starbucks Coffee Canada Inc (2005, 2006, 2009)
- Suncor Energy Inc. (2005)
- TD Canada Trust (2007)
- TELUS (2009)
- The Home Depot Canada (2010)
- The Princess Margaret Hospital Foundation (Broader Public Sector, 2010)
- Tim Hortons (2005, 2006, 2007, 2008)
- Walmart Canada (2009)
- WestJet (2005, 2006, 2007, 2008)
- Whole Foods Market (The Green Award, 2009)
- Workopolis (Best Emerging Organization, 2009)
- Yellow Pages Group (2005, 2006, 2007, 2008)

Notes

Chapter 1
1. Waterstone Human Capital, "Canada's 10 Most Admired Corporate Cultures of 2010".
2. Maple Leaf Foods, "Purdy Crawford Appointed as Chairman", news release, June 29, 2011, investor.mapleleaf.ca.
3. Maple Leaf Foods, "What Is Six Sigma at Maple Leaf?" Six Sigma Careers, mapleleaf.ca.
4. Maple Leaf Foods, "Our Food Safety Action Plan", Food Safety, mapleleaf.ca.
5. Maple Leaf Foods, "Maple Leaf Foods Reports Third Quarter Financial Results", news release, October 28, 2009, investor .mapleleaf.ca.
6. "Restructuring at Maple Leaf Foods Putting Share Values Back on Track: McCain", April 28, 2011, GuelphMercury.com.
7. Four Seasons Hotels and Resorts, "About Us", fourseasons.com.
8. Isadore Sharp, *Four Seasons: The Story of a Business Philosophy* (Toronto: Penguin Group, 2009), pp. 93, 99.
9. "Leadership Lessons from Isadore Sharp", *Career Insider Business*, 2011, careerinsiderbusiness.ca.
10. Sharp, *Four Seasons*, p. 106.
11. Ibid., pp. 285–289.

Chapter 2

1. WestJet Investor Fact Sheet and "About WestJet", westjet.com.
2. "Boston Pizza's Three Pillars of Success", Boston Pizza Quick Facts, bostonpizza.com.

Chapter 3

1. Acklands-Grainger Inc., "About Us", acklandsgrainger.com.
2. Acklands-Grainger Inc., "Company History", acklandsgrainger.com.
3. Court Carruthers, Corporate Culture Summit, "The Power of Culture in International Growth", February 7, 2010.
4. Acklands-Grainger Inc., "Company History".
5. Acklands-Grainger Inc., submission to "Canada's 10 Most Admired Corporate Cultures of 2009", Waterstone Human Capital.
6. Maple Leaf Foods, submission to "Canada's 10 Most Admired Corporate Cultures of 2010", Waterstone Human Capital.
7. Interview with Wayne Johnson, (retired) senior vice president and chief human resources officer, Maple Leaf Foods, 2009.
8. Yellow Media Inc., "About Us/Company Profile", ypg.com.
9. Agrium Inc., "What We Do", agrium.com.
10. Interview with Mike Wilson, CEO, and Jim Gossett, senior vice president of human resources, Agrium, April 2011.
11. Healthcare of Ontario Pension Plan (HOOPP), "At a Glance—A HOOPP Fact Sheet", hoopp.com.
12. Healthcare of Ontario Pension Plan, submission to "Canada's 10 Most Admired Corporate Cultures of 2010", Waterstone Human Capital.
13. Healthcare of Ontario Pension Plan, 2010 Annual Report.
14. Agrium Inc., submission to "Canada's 10 Most Admired Corporate Cultures of 2010", Waterstone Human Capital.
15. Direct Energy, submission to Canada's 10 Most Admired Corporate Cultures of 2011", Waterstone Human Capital.
16. Acklands-Grainger Inc., submission to "Canada's 10 Most Admired Corporate Cultures of 2009", Waterstone Human Capital.
17. Coastal Contacts, submission to "Canada's 10 Most Admired Corporate Cultures of 2010", Waterstone Human Capital.

18. Shoppers Drug Mart, submission to "Canada's 10 Most Admired Corporate Cultures of 2011", Waterstone Human Capital.
19. Interview with Darren Entwistle, CEO, and Josh Blair, executive vice president, human resources, TELUS, July 2011.
20. Tim Hortons, "Corporate Profile", timhortons.com.
21. Tim Hortons Children's Foundation, submission to "Canada's 10 Most Admired Corporate Cultures of 2010", Waterstone Human Capital.
22. "Marathon of Hope Continues around the World", livingvalues.fourseasons.com.
23. "Canadian Breast Cancer Foundation CIBC Run for the Cure", cibc.com.
24. Interview with Clive Beddoe, founding shareholder and chairman, WestJet, March 2011.

Chapter 4
1. Princess Margaret Hospital Foundation, submission to "Canada's 10 Most Admired Corporate Cultures of 2010", Waterstone Human Capital.
2. Ibid.
3. Paul Alofs, president and CEO, Sherri Freedman, chief development officer, and Christine Lasky, vice president, strategic initiatives, Princess Margaret Hospital Foundation, "Building a Transformational Culture—Lessons from Social Enterprise", Corporate Culture Summit, February 2011.
4. Ibid.

Chapter 5
1. Maple Leaf Foods, submission to "Canada's 10 Most Admired Corporate Cultures of 2010", Waterstone Human Capital.
2. Ibid.
3. "Jumpstart—These Kids Wear Crowns," Official Coastal Contacts Lip Dub Video, 2011.
4. Schlegel Villages, "The Schlegel Organizational Culture".

Chapter 6

1. Right to Play, submission to "Canada's 10 Most Admired Corporate Cultures of 2011", Waterstone Human Capital.
2. Waterstone Human Capital, "2011 Canadian Corporate Culture Study".
3. Kinross, submission to "Canada's 10 Most Admired Corporate Cultures of 2011", Waterstone Human Capital.
4. Herminia Ibarra, "Making Partner: A Mentor's Guide to the Psychological Journey," *Harvard Business Review* 78, no. 2, 2000.
5. Interview with Wayne Johnson, (retired) senior vice president and chief human resources officer, Maple Leaf Foods, 2009.

Chapter 7

1. CCL Group, "About CCL Group", cclgroup.ca.
2. "Marathon of Hope Continues around the World", livingvalues .fourseasons.com; "Isadore Sharp", fourseasons.com.

Chapter 8

1. Johnson & Johnson, "Company Structure", jnj.com.
2. Johnson & Johnson, "Our Credo", jnj.com.
3. Judith Rehak, "Tylenol Made a Hero of Johnson & Johnson: The Recall That Started Them All", *New York Times*, March 23, 2002.
4. Isadore Sharp, *Four Seasons: The Story of a Business Philosophy* (Toronto: Penguin Group, 2009), p. 106.

Chapter 9

1. John P. Kotter and James L. Heskett, *Corporate Culture and Performance* (New York: Free Press, 1992).

Chapter 10

1. Waterstone Human Capital, "2011 Canadian Corporate Culture Study".
2. Ibid.
3. Yellow Media Inc., "About Us/Company Profile", ypg.com.
4. Yellow Media Inc., "About Us/History—A Long Tradition of Leadership", ypg.com; and Marc Tellier, president and CEO of

YPG, Trader, and Canpages, "Culture Change at YPG", Corporate Culture Summit, February 2010.
5. Tellier, Presentation.
6. Waterstone, "2011 Canadian Corporate Culture Study".
7. Ibid.
8. Theresa Tedesco and Matt Hartley, "What Went Wrong at RIM?" *Financial Post*, July 12, 2011.

Chapter 11

1. Acklands-Grainger Inc., "Our Offering" and "About Us", acklands grainger.com.
2. Interview with Court Carruthers, senior vice president, Grainger, and president, Grainger International, and Sean O'Brien, president, Acklands-Grainger, 2011.
3. Edgar H. Schein, *The Corporate Culture Survival Guide* (Hoboken, N.J.: John Wiley & Sons, 2009), pp. 105–122.
4. Yellow Media Inc., "About Us/History—A Long Tradition of Leadership", ypg.com.
5. Yellow Media Inc., "About Us/Management Team—Marc P. Tellier", ypg.com.
6. Yellow Media, "History".
7. Marc Tellier, president and CEO of YPG, Trader, and Canpages, "Culture Change at YPG", Corporate Culture Summit, February 2010.
8. Jim Collins, *Good to Great: Why Some Companies Make the Leap . . . and Others Don't* (New York: HarperCollins, 2001), p. 39.

Chapter 13

1. Carolyn Clark, senior vice president, human resources, Fairmont Hotels and Resorts, panel presentation, "The Power of Culture in International Growth," Corporate Culture Summit, February 2011.
2. Coastal Contacts, "Coastal Contacts Sets New Eyeglasses Orders Record of $2.0 Million Last Week", news release, March 23, 2011, investors.coastalcontacts.com.
3. Ibid.

4. Interview with Mike Wilson, CEO, and Jim Grossett, senior vice president of human resources, Agrium, 2011.

Chapter 14

1. Maple Leaf Foods, submission to "Canada's 10 Most Admired Corporate Cultures of 2010", Waterstone Human Capital.
2. Maple Leaf Foods, "Maple Leaf Governance", investor .mapleleaf.ca.
3. Tim Hortons, "Tim Hortons Inc. Board Commences CEO Search; Executive Chairman Paul House Appointed Interim CEO," news release, May 25, 2011, timhortons.com.

Chapter 15

1. TELUS, "About Us—Strategies and Values", telus.com.
2. Interview with Darren Entwistle, CEO, and Josh Blair, executive vice president of human resources, TELUS, July 2011.
3. Bill Taylor, "Why We (Shouldn't) Hate HR", *Harvard Business Review Blog Network*, June 10, 2010.
4. TELUS, "TELUS CEO Darren Entwistle to Be Honoured with Fraser Institute's T. Patrick Boyle Founder's Award", news release, April 28, 2011, telus.com.
5. David Ulrich and Wendy Ulrich, *The Why of Work: How Great Leaders Build Abundant Organizations* (New York: McGraw-Hill, 2010).
6. "Elisabetta Bigsby Retires from RBC", rbc.com.

Chapter 16

1. Waterstone Human Capital, "2011 Canadian Corporate Culture Study".
2. Ibid.
3. Ibid.

Chapter 18

1. Interview with Darren Entwistle, CEO, and Josh Blair, executive vice president, human resources, TELUS, July 2011.

2. TELUS, "TELUS CEO Darren Entwistle to Be Honoured with Fraser Institute's T. Patrick Boyle Founder's Award", news release, April 28, 2011, telus.com.

3. Four Seasons Hotels and Resorts, "Corporate Bios—Isadore Sharp", fourseasons.com.

4. Four Seasons Hotels and Resorts, "About Us", fourseasons.com.

5. "The Golden Rule—An Interview with Katie Taylor, President and Chief Executive Officer, Four Seasons Hotels and Resorts", *Leaders Magazine* 34, no. 1, 2011.

6. "Creating Memorable Customer Experiences Help Lumière & Four Seasons Resort Whistler Land Exclusive AAA/CAA Five Diamond Awards", British Columbia Automobile Association news release, January 14, 2011, cnw.ca.

7. Interview with Court Carruthers, senior vice president, Grainger, and president, Grainger International, and Sean O'Brien, president, Acklands-Grainger, 2011.

8. Ibid.

9. Ibid.

10. Interview with Marc Tellier, president and CEO of YPG, Trader, and Canpages, October 2010.

11. Yellow Media Inc., "Q1 Fact Sheet", May 2011.

12. Ibid.

13. Waterstone Human Capital, Canada's 10 Most Admired Corporate Cultures Hall of Fame Video, February 2010.

14. WestJet Investor Fact Sheet.

15. WestJet, submission to "Canada's 10 Most Admired Corporate Cultures of 2011", Waterstone Human Capital.

16. WestJet Investor Fact Sheet.

17. WestJet, submission to "Canada's 10 Most Admired Corporate Cultures of 2011".

18. Waterstone, Hall of Fame Video, February 2010.

19. Tim Hortons, "Tim Hortons Inc. Board Commences CEO Search; Executive Chairman Paul House Appointed Interim CEO," news release, May 25, 2011, timhortons.com; and interview with Paul House, executive chairman, Tim Hortons, and Brigid Pelino, senior vice president of human resources, Tim Hortons, July 2011.

20. Tim Hortons, "Tim Hortons Inc. Board Commences CEO Search".
21. Tim Hortons Inc., 2010 Annual Report.
22. Ibid.
23. Interview with Carolyn Clark, senior vice president of human resources, Fairmont Hotels and Resorts, June 2011.
24. Fairmont Hotels and Resorts, "Company Facts", fairmont.com.
25. "Fairmont amongst the 'World's Best'", July 13, 2011, fairmont.com; and "Awards and Accolades", fairmont.com.
26. Interview with E. Hunter Harrison, (retired) president and CEO, CN, and Les Dakens, (retired) vice president, human resources, CN, June 2010.
27. E. Hunter Harrison, (retired) president and CEO, CN, and Les Dakens, (retired) vice president, human resources, CN, "Culture Change at CN", Waterstone Human Capital, June 2010.
28. Ibid.
29. Waterstone Human Capital, "Canada's 10 Most Admired Corporate Cultures of 2010".
30. Ibid.
31. Ibid.
32. Waterstone Human Capital, "2011 Canadian Corporate Culture Study".
33. Ibid.
34. Ibid.
35. Ibid.
36. Ibid.
37. Ibid.
38. Isadore Sharp, *Four Seasons: The Story of a Business Philosophy* (Toronto: Penguin Group, 2009), p. xvi.

Index

About the Author

Marty Parker is chairman and chief executive offi-
cer of Waterstone Human Capital. Marty is the
country's leading expert on human capital, and is
a frequent commentator on issues surrounding corporate leadership and organizational culture. He
has written for the *National Post, Canadian Business* and *Profit,* and has appeared on Canada AM,
BNN and CP24. He also publishes a regular
newsletter called *The Waterline: Highs and Lows
in Leadership and Corporate Culture.*

Marty founded Waterstone Human Capital—a leading retained
executive search firm specializing in recruiting for fit and in cultural
assessment—in 2003. In 2005, he founded Canada's 10 Most Admired
Corporate Cultures, an annual national program now in its seventh year.
Canada's 10 recognizes best-in-class Canadian organizations for having a
culture that has helped them enhance performance and sustain a competitive advantage.

Formerly, Marty was managing director and partner with The Cald-
well Partners International, and was executive vice-president of The CCL
Group, a leading marketing communications group of companies.
His earlier career was with Johnson & Johnson and Labatt Breweries,
where he held progressively senior sales and marketing positions.

Marty is a member of the Young Presidents' Organization and the
Entrepreneurs' Organization and is a former director of VON Canada
and Junior Achievement. He holds a Bachelor of Arts as well as a Master
of Science from the University of Guelph.